T0328686

Cambridge Elements ≡

Elements in Epistemology
edited by
Stephen Hetherington
University of New South Wales, Sydney

PHILOSOPHY, BULLSHIT, AND PEER REVIEW

Neil Levy
Macquarie University and the University of Oxford

CAMBRIDGE
UNIVERSITY PRESS

Shaftesbury Road, Cambridge CB2 8EA, United Kingdom

One Liberty Plaza, 20th Floor, New York, NY 10006, USA

477 Williamstown Road, Port Melbourne, VIC 3207, Australia

314–321, 3rd Floor, Plot 3, Splendor Forum, Jasola District Centre, New Delhi – 110025, India

103 Penang Road, #05–06/07, Visioncrest Commercial, Singapore 238467

Cambridge University Press is part of Cambridge University Press & Assessment, a department of the University of Cambridge.

We share the University's mission to contribute to society through the pursuit of education, learning and research at the highest international levels of excellence.

www.cambridge.org
Information on this title: www.cambridge.org/9781009462310

DOI: 10.1017/9781009256315

First published 2023

A catalogue record for this publication is available from the British Library

ISBN 978-1-009-46231-0 Hardback
ISBN 978-1-009-25630-8 Paperback
ISSN 2398-0567 (online)
ISSN 2514-3832 (print)

Philosophy, Bullshit, and Peer Review

Elements in Epistemology

DOI: 10.1017/9781009256315
First published online: December 2023

Neil Levy
Macquarie University and the University of Oxford
Author for correspondence: Neil Levy, Neil.levy@mq.edu.au

Abstract: Peer review is supposed to ensure that published work, in philosophy and in other disciplines, meets high standards of rigor and interest. But many people fear that it is no longer fit to play this role. This Element examines some of their concerns. It uses evidence that critics of peer review sometimes cite to show its failures, as well as empirical literature on the reception of bullshit, to advance positive claims about how the assessment of scholarly work is appropriately influenced by features of the context in which it appears: for example, by readers' knowledge of authorship or of publication venue. Reader attitude makes an appropriate and sometimes decisive difference to perceptions of argument quality. The Element ends by considering the difference that authors' attitudes to their own arguments can appropriately make to their reception. This title is also available as Open Access on Cambridge Core.

Keywords: peer review, bullshit, academic hoaxes, prestige bias, trust

ISBNs: 9781009462310 (HB), 9781009256308 (PB), 9781009256315 (OC)
ISSNs: 2398-0567 (online), 2514-3832 (print)

Contents

Introduction

Kant identified three questions that philosophy must address: What can I know? What must I do? What may I hope? Today, a fourth question preoccupies many philosophers: Why was my paper rejected? Philosophers, and academics in many other disciplines, pore over reports from reviewers and editors, shaking their heads in disgust. Why didn't they recognize the brilliance of my ideas? Who thought *that* clown was competent to review my paper? I'm going to argue that answering these sorts of questions – questions concerning how reviewers evaluate the papers they consider, and what influences their decisions – requires us to get to grips with the factors that modulate intellectual charity.

The narrower goal of this Element is to shed some light on peer review, and in particular on some of the evidence for the widespread feeling that peer review is broken.[1] It will focus, in particular, on the evidence arising from the sometimes widely disparate responses competent readers might have to the same paper. A number of theorists have pointed to the fact that papers subsequently regarded as groundbreaking were rejected multiple times before finally finding a home, and to empirical evidence that accepted papers do not fare particularly well when resubmitted with cosmetic changes, and concluded that peer review doesn't do a good job at tracking quality. I will argue that though this evidence does show that what gets published is somewhat arbitrary, it does not show that journals don't do a reasonable job at selecting excellent papers.

The broader goal of the Element is to understand the difference that attitudes – those of readers, of reviewers, and of authors themselves – do and should make to the assessment of texts (whether journal articles or books). I will argue for a counterintuitive thesis: the quality of a paper (or a book: texts more generally) is not wholly intrinsic to it, but is a partly relational property – it depends in part on contextual factors. Context modulates the attitude we take to a paper, and that attitude, in turn, helps to shape our perception of its value. We can't use the history of a paper as a metric by which to assess its unchanging value, because its value is *not* unchanging before and after publication. Publication is one among many factors that (rationally) affect our perception of a paper's quality. Who wrote it, where it is published, what others have, or have not, said about it – all these, too, make a difference to our rational perception of its quality.

In Sections 1 and 2 of this Element, I will examine how intra- and extratextual features of texts affect reviewer attitudes toward them. In Sections 3 and 4, I will broaden the focus, to include the role that reader and author attitudes can and should play in modulating the perceived quality of a text. In Section 3, I ask

---

[1] The phrase "peer review is broken" returned about 321,000 hits on Google (as of December 11, 2022).

whether reviewers should be less trusting of the intentions of authors, in the light of recent attempts to hoax journals. I'll argue that such wariness is corrosive. Academic research is heavily reliant on trust, and we risk important goods if we become less trusting. In the final section, I will turn from the attitudes of reviewers and subsequent readers to the attitudes of authors, asking what attitudes we permissibly take to the claims we make in our own papers. I'll suggest that *assessor* attitude is partially a response to perceived *author* attitude: we permissibly modulate trust and intellectual charity by indicating our own degree of commitment to our claims (we may also mislead to the same effect, of course). In short, paper quality does not depend exclusively on the arguments presented but also on the attitude of assessors, and these attitudes can be modulated by many factors including the attitude the author is perceived to take to them.[2]

These claims – that quality is partially a relational property, that assessor attitude makes a difference to perceived quality, and that attitude is rationally modulated by a range of intra- and extratextual factors – are true well beyond philosophy. They're probably somewhat less true with regard to formal and deductive arguments than those which are inductive or abductive, but they play a role everywhere. This is a work *of* philosophy, and philosophy is the discipline I know best, so I will focus on it, but the issues I'll consider arise in other disciplines too. Wherever people are in the business of assessing one another's work, explicitly or implicitly (for example, by choosing to cite *this* paper, rather than *that*), they arise. I'll have little to say about these other disciplines, though: the implications will usually be clear.

It's important to emphasize that this Element is concerned with only a narrow slice of the evidence against peer review: the evidence that arises from the (erroneous) assumption that paper quality is a wholly intrinsic property. There are many concerns it leaves aside, and some may motivate the replacement of peer review by some other system. It's equally important, though, to recognize that assessor attitude will continue to play a role in perceptions of quality under any proposed replacement for peer review. So long as we're in the business of making distinctions on the basis of quality, the considerations I'll discuss will be relevant. Of course, assessing work on the basis of quality is something we can't avoid doing. We often need to settle how much weight to give to the claims of

---

[2] It bears noting that the basic view defended in this Element is in some ways parallel to, and may in fact be inspired by, the account of interpretation famously developed by Hans-Georg Gadamer (1975). To my knowledge, Gadamer never applied his framework to the kinds of issues I consider here. I'm not sufficiently versed in his views to assess the degree to which my account departs from his.

a book or paper, and answering that question inevitably involves assessing its quality.

Before beginning the exploration of the difference that attitude rationally makes to perceptions of quality, a brief explanation of the focus on peer review, and on its nature, might be in order. It's important, first, to emphasize the *centrality* of peer review, both to the professional lives of philosophers (and researchers in many other fields) and to the growth of knowledge. The stakes are high for individuals. The journal article is the principal unit of publication in professional philosophy (as in most, though not all, academic disciplines), and a solid record of publication in journals is almost always needed for professional success. Hiring decisions are made on the basis of candidates' publication records, and tenure requires continuing publication. Grants and self-esteem are also dependent on track record.

Peer review is also widely regarded as playing an important *epistemic* role. It is supposed to act as a guarantor that research was well-conducted, and that findings are reliable enough to be taken seriously. Anyone can publish their arguments and their research. Anyone can make a website, and if one wants one's writing to appear in journal format, there are plenty of predatory journals that will publish anything for a fee. But if one wants to be taken seriously, it's important to publish in a properly peer-reviewed journal.

The professional centrality and epistemic significance of peer review both reflect the fact that it's widely held to be a reliable measure of the quality of research. Peer review is usually *anonymous*. Review is usually either single or double anonymous. In single anonymous review, reviewers know the identity of the author(s) but not vice-versa; reviewers are therefore free to be honest without fearing retaliation or worrying about maintaining good relations with authors. In double anonymous review, reviewers and authors are both anonymous: this is often held to be superior to single anonymous review because it ensures that reviewers will not be swayed by the prestige (or lack thereof) of the author(s).

While peer review is widely held to be especially reliable at identifying quality, peer-reviewed journals are not all created equal. Some are more prestigious than others. Philosophers, like other academics, take the prestige of a journal into account when choosing where to submit their papers. Journal choice is guided by "fit" – different journals focus on different areas within philosophy, as well as taking different approaches – and prestige. Generally speaking, a philosopher will aim for the most prestigious journal they think might possibly take their paper. She will almost certainly be sensitive to journal prestige (within her subfield, or within the profession as a whole), regardless of whether she believes that prestige genuinely correlates with quality. The unemployed and insecurely employed know that prestige publications boost their chances of secure employment and the untenured know that such publications may be required for tenure. Prestige publications are also required for securing grants. And, rightly or wrongly, almost all of us are motivated by a desire for recognition: the fact that many of their peers think more highly of work published in prestige journals motivates philosophers to try to publish in them.

But the more prestigious the journal, the lower the acceptance rate: the competition is intense and the stakes are high. While accurate and up-to-date information is hard to come by, the median acceptance rate in philosophy seems to be substantially lower than in most other fields (Weinberg, 2018). The acceptance rates for the most competitive philosophy journals, like *Ethics* (Driver and Rosati, 2021) and *Philosophical Review* (Philosophical Review, 2022) are lower than the rates for *Science* (Science, 2022) and *Nature* (Nature, 2021). Not only is the competition for the top spots more intense, the number of prestigious outlets is relatively small. Almost every respectable journal rejects most of the submissions it receives; many in philosophy reject upward of 90 percent of submissions. When the rejection is accompanied by one or more reviewer reports (desk rejection – rejection by the editors without peer review – is not unusual), we often read these reports obsessively. We may take to social media to slam them. There's a Facebook group called "Reviewer 2 Must be Stopped!," where academics go to vent about the perceived (and sometimes actual) ineptitude of reviewers (Reviewer 2 is the proverbially unfair, obtuse, rude, and often incompetent reviewer). The group has nearly 75,000 members, so we can be confident that obsession with bad reports is common across many disciplines. Sometimes reports are very helpful and illuminating (sometimes, they've even convinced me that the journal was right to reject my paper). Sometimes, they're incompetent. Mostly, they fall somewhere in between these extremes.

No one doubts that peer review is far from perfect. Papers that shouldn't have been published get through far more often than they should, and many, many good papers are rejected (whether that's a failing in need of rectification is one of the questions I'm concerned with here). There are now serious ongoing debates over its value. Peer review is now regarded as the gold standard for scientific credibility. Yet its dominance is surprisingly recent. *Science* (founded in 1880) introduced it around 1940; *The Lancet* (1823) only in 1976 (Shema, 2014). Prior to its introduction, journals relied on editors' opinions to select papers for publication. Science without peer review is certainly possible, and many researchers have proposed alternatives to the current system that would reduce or eliminate some of its failures (at minimum, by reducing or eliminating the lengthy delays, and therefore opportunity costs, it involves). We might for instance adopt the model already dominant in some parts of physics: postpublication review (Heesen and Bright, 2020). This model abolishes journals altogether or places much less weight on publication in them. Instead, papers are uploaded to a preprint server, and it is their reception by the community of scholars that determines their success.

Perhaps we *should* replace peer review. I won't attempt to assess the issue here. In the end, I'm concerned not with peer review per se, but with epistemic issues in the assessment of the kind of work that gets peer reviewed, whatever the context in which that assessment occurs. I don't apologize for framing the issue around peer review, however, because (right now) it is in peer review that the most consequential assessment takes place, and because the considerations I'll highlight bear quite directly on some of the evidence for the claim that peer review is broken. Recognizing the difference that attitude can make to our justified assessment of a paper, and how attitude responds rationally to intra- and extratextual features beyond the argument and the data, can help to defuse some of the anger peer review arouses. In the concluding section, I'll argue that it also alerts us to some of the trade-offs, between different epistemic goods and between epistemic and nonepistemic goods, we face in designing any refinements to or replacement of peer review.

I'm going to begin in what might seem a surprising place: by plunging into bullshit, and the literature that discusses it. Section 1 will examine this literature, with an eye to understanding why we sometimes call bullshit on texts. Section 2 will apply the lessons learned to peer review. Understanding bullshit will provide us with tools that can be used to understand more nuanced and sympathetic assessments of philosophical work. By wading through the bullshit, we'll come to appreciate the decisive difference that intellectual charity routinely and inevitably plays in our assessments. These sections establish (to my satisfaction, at any rate) that attitude can make a decisive difference in our assessment of texts. Sections 3 and 4 inquire into the attitudes we justifiably take to texts, first as reviewers (Section 3), then as authors (Section 4).

1 Bullshit Philosophy

Why tread in bullshit? One reason might be because philosophy itself is often dismissed as bullshit. Perhaps understanding the nature of bullshit, or the disposition to attribute it, might help us to defend it against the accusation. I have a different goal in mind, however. I'm going to argue that understanding the conditions under which we're tempted to attribute bullshit sheds light on the ways in which our attitudes affect our assessment of one another's papers. The attribution of bullshit to an assertion or a text generally arises from a lack of intellectual charity in reading. Reviewers rarely withhold intellectual charity to such an extent that they're tempted to see the papers they review as bullshit, but – I'm going to claim – much smaller differences in intellectual charity can and do explain much smaller (but still often decisive) differences in the assessment of papers. They may, for example, make the difference between "reject" and "revise and resubmit." We'll be better able to appreciate the smaller differences attitude makes, in peer review, for example, once we've seen how it can transform the tolerably clear into the incomprehensible.

The inquiry into bullshit will also guide us in identifying the kind of factors that modulate attitudes. Calling bullshit is, in paradigm cases, a response to both intra- and extratextual cues – in particular, cues that suggest the genre it belongs to. In subsequent sections, we'll identify other cues that play similar roles in modulating assessor attitudes.

1.1 Understanding Bullshit

The accusation that philosophy is bullshit is common (the phrase "philosophy is bullshit" returns more than 39,000 results on Google). Eminent scientists like Stephen Hawking, and influential science popularizers like Neil DeGrasse Tyson and Bill Nye have dismissed its value (Goldhill, 2016). Philosophers themselves are often ready to denigrate particular areas or approaches as bullshit, or something equivalent to bullshit. Dismissals of all or parts of "continental philosophy" as bullshit are not at all uncommon, though thankfully rarer now than in the past. The name-calling is by no means one-sided: Graham Harman is scarcely more charitable when he decries the "shallowness, false dichotomies, lack of imagination, robotic chains of reasoning, and the aggressive self-assurance that typifies analytic philosophers at their worst"; lest you think he reserves his scorn only for some pockets of analytic philosophy, he adds "we need to question the assumptions of this entire school" (Harman, 2009: 167–168). But the accusation that a school of philosophy is bullshit is reserved for "difficult" and "obscure" work. Even if we think that the kind of philosophy characterized by numbered premises, formal proofs, and attempts at exceptionless definitions is arid and sterile, we're unlikely to dismiss it as bullshit.

Is (some) philosophy bullshit? Harry Frankfurt (2009) has influentially argued that bullshit consists in assertions made without regard to whether they're true. If that's what's meant when some people dismiss some schools of philosophy as bullshit, it's often question-begging: it begs the question against those schools that aim at bringing us to see the world differently, rather than at stating truths about it. It might be true that some philosophers don't care whether what they're saying is literally true, but it doesn't follow – without a lot of argument – that their work deserves to be dismissed as bullshit. Just as importantly, sincerity doesn't guarantee that an assertion isn't bullshit. Think of the accusation "he believes his own bullshit"; if Frankfurt-style bullshit was the only kind there was, that accusation would make little sense.

Frankfurt's account also doesn't capture how "bullshit" is used in the empirical literature. This literature builds on Gordon Pennycook and colleagues' (2015) path-breaking work. They define "bullshit" in terms of form and content, rather than the attitudes of those who produce it: on their account, bullshit consists in assertions that, in virtue of their syntactic structure, seem to convey meaning but (supposedly) lack genuine content. Their paradigms are the obscure sayings of the purveyors of supposed new age wisdom, like this example they draw from Deepak Chopra: "Attention and intention are the mechanics of manifestation" (Pennycook *et al.*, 2015: 550). Their interest as psychologists is in what characteristics of hearers or readers make them receptive to these assertions; that is, what are the psychological correlates of finding bullshit profound?

Pennycook *et al.* take their account of bullshit to pick out assertions that also count as Frankfurt-bullshit, but they're wrong about that. Deepak Chopra may or may not be indifferent to whether his assertions are true. His attitude is irrelevant to whether they *are* bullshit, on their account. Gerry Cohen (2013) has offered an alternative account, which seems better able to capture what Pennycook *et al.* call "pseudo-profound bullshit." Cohen doesn't aim to replace Frankfurt's notion; rather, he argues that we need more than one account to capture all the bullshit that's out there. Cohen-style bullshit can be sincerely intended; its distinguishing mark is that it's "unclarifiable" (Cohen, 2013: 104).

Cohen also brings the discussion directly back to philosophy: he singles out "Francophone philosophical culture" as the "most successful producer of bullshit, both in respect of the volume of bullshit that it has produced and in respect of the warmth with which that bullshit has been received" (Cohen, 2013: 108). Again, Cohen doesn't dispute that those who produce the work he mentions (Deleuze, Derrida, Kristeva, and Lacan, as well as the Althusserian Marxists who are his special target) are sincere. He thinks they aim at truth, at least truth of a kind. Nevertheless, what they say is *not* true: it's not even false.

Cohen's original interest in bullshit stems from an avowedly autobiographical motivation. In his twenties, he tells us, he read a great deal of French Marxism, most of it stemming from the Althusserian school. He goes on to report that he struggled to extract meaning from these texts, and when he was able to make some sense of them attributed more significance to the claims than they really deserved, in virtue of the effort he'd expended extracting them. His dalliance with Althusserian Marxism subsequently made him intolerant of bullshit, and when he founded a Marxist discussion group he called it the Non-Bullshit Marxism Group (Cohen, 2013: 95). We'll return to Cohen's confessed intolerance of bullshit; I think his preconceptions about these texts matter a great deal to his responses to them. In any case, his principal example – his "wonderful example of bullshit" – comes from a former student of Althusser's, Étienne Balibar: "This is precisely the first meaning we can give to the idea of dialectic: a logic or form of explanation specifically adapted to the determinant intervention of class struggle in the very fabric of history" (Balibar, 2014: 97). Cohen might once have assessed Balibar's assertion as profound; he now dismisses it as bullshit. Can the psychological work shed light on why he was once impressed, and perhaps on why he is now dismissive?

Pennycook *et al.* (2015) asked their participants to rate the assertions they were presented with – drawn from Deepak Chopra's tweets and from two online new age bullshit generators – for profundity, alongside motivational quotes and mundane assertions. They found that bullshit receptivity was correlated with an intuitive cognitive style and lower cognitive ability, as well as with higher rates of religious and paranormal belief. Allegedly, people are impressed by bullshit due to their failure or inability to detect the vacuity of the stimuli. I think it's vanishingly unlikely that Cohen fits their model, in cognitive style, in ability, or in beliefs in the supernatural. Perhaps another account of bullshit receptivity might do better at explaining his dalliance with Althusserian Marxism?

The empirical literature can be mined for other explanations. Pennycook *et al.* (2015) probed the interaction between the (allegedly nonsensical) content of the assertions that feature as stimuli in their work and the dispositions of those who are receptive to them. Other work looks instead to the apparent *source* of assertions (as well as their content) to explain receptiveness. Dan Sperber (2010) has identified the *guru effect*, whereby high credibility is assigned to an assertion in virtue of the fact that it is obscure *and* it is believed to stem from someone who is a "guru"; that is, a source of wisdom. Sperber takes the guru effect to partly explain the success of some philosophers, "especially but not uniquely in the so-called continental tradition" (Sperber, 2010: 587); Sperber goes on to quote Sartre, Heidegger, and Derrida; perhaps Balibar could be added to Sperber's list.

More recently, the guru effect has been joined by the *Einstein effect* (Hoogeveen *et al.*, 2022). In this study, stimuli generated by the New-Age Bullshit Generator[3] were attributed to either a scientist or a spiritual leader.

---

[3] http://sebpearce.com/bullshit/.

Across more than 10,000 participants in 24 countries, assertions were judged as more credible when attributed to a scientist than to a spiritual leader; even religious participants tended to see statements attributed to a scientist as more credible than identical statements attributed to a spiritual authority. Perhaps the success of bullshit in Francophone philosophy is due to the special status of philosophers in France: because they have the status of "gurus," their nonsense is attributed with a great deal of credibility, despite – or perhaps in virtue of – its "unclarifiability."

The source and content effects just listed – the guru effect, the Einstein effect, the effects of bullshit on perceptions of profundity – are typically conceived as different ways in which assertions are given an underserved boost in credibility in the eyes of those who are susceptible. The credibility inflation is held to be undeserved, because – after all – the statements that are rated as credible and even profound are designed to be *meaningless*. The bullshit receptivity scale developed by Pennycook *et al.* (2015: supplementary material) uses items like the following: "We are in the midst of a high-frequency blossoming of interconnectedness that will give us access to the quantum soup itself." The Einstein effect was measured using stimuli like: "Yes, it is possible to exterminate the things that can confront us, but not without hope on our side. Turbulence is born in the gap where transformation has been excluded. It is in evolving that we are re-energized" (Hoogeveen *et al.*, 2022: supplementary material). Since these are bullshit statements, the assignment of *any* degree of credibility and profundity to them is undeserved.

Of course, credibility boosts in virtue of these kinds of effects might often attach to genuinely meaningful statements too: they might be perceived as more profound than they deserve, given their relatively banal contents. Meaningful statements can have their credibility boosted in still other ways. Several studies have found that the use of irrelevant neuroscientific information boosts the credibility of assertions for naïve participants (Weisberg *et al.*, 2008; Fernandez-Duque, Evans, and Hodges, 2015). There's no reason to think that these kinds of effects are limited to extraneous neuroscientific information. Scientific jargon of all sorts probably impresses many people.

Cohen may have briefly fallen victim to the guru effect or the Einstein effect: the status of the philosopher within France may have led him to take Balibar's claims to be more significant than they deserve. In doing so, he would have fallen victim to what I'm calling an *extratextual* influence: his assessment of the text was influenced by awareness of facts outside the text. Alternatively, he may have been moved by *intratextual* factors: for example, the obscurity of the claims. Of course, these kinds of influences interact and are rarely cleanly separated. The content of a new age aphorism suggests a "spiritual leader" as its source; conversely, banal assertions from a scientist get little or no boost in credibility in virtue of their source. One way or another, Cohen was taken in by bullshit, or so he later came to think.

1.2 Deserving Bullshit

With these tools in hand, we can now put fine clothes on our resentments. We analytic philosophers, with our careful arguments and our rigor and our devotion to clarity, are outshone in the public eye by continental philosophers who disguise their essential triviality under layers of apparently significant pseudo-profundity. Their claims, when they bother to make them, are either devoid of meaning altogether, or cover essentially mundane thoughts with an unearned glamour (Shackel, 2005). We may not be able to partake of their aura, but at least we have the satisfaction of exposing them for what they are, and laying bare the tricks that take in the unwary.

None of this is true. Whatever the merits of continental philosophy – or particular strands within it – the empirical work on bullshit does not provide us with any grounds for dismissing or downgrading it. It might be true that the work of (some) continental philosophers receives a credibility boost in virtue of features of their content that might be paraphrased away without loss of meaning, or in virtue of the status of the intellectual, and specifically the philosopher, in France. But it's not true that any such credibility boost is strictly extraneous or necessarily undeserved. It may be fully rational to assign a higher degree of credibility to a text (with "text," understood broadly, to encompass anything from an assertion through to a corpus of work) in virtue of features of its content that could be paraphrased away, or of its apparent source.

This is clearest with regard to the Einstein effect. It should be entirely obvious that we do and *should* assign higher credibility to assertions by scientists speaking in their domain of expertise, in virtue of the fact that they issue from scientists. We're rarely in a position to verify scientific claims for ourselves; instead, we accept the claims of specialists speaking within the domain of their expertise because we take them to be much better positioned to make such claims than we are. It's worth emphasizing how routine this kind of deference is, especially in light of the politicization of science that was a central feature of the COVID-19 pandemic (and which led many people to doubt the epistemic credentials of epidemiologists). We may not automatically accept the diagnoses of medical professionals, but we almost always assign high credibility to them, in virtue of the fact that they have a medical degree. If the stakes are high enough, or if we have some reason to doubt the professional, we might seek a second opinion. But we (most of us, at any rate) don't look beyond the domain of medical expertise: we turn to *another* medical professional, in recognition of their domain-specific credibility.

The phenomenon is by no means restricted to medical professionals. We assign especially high credibility to scientists speaking in the domain of their expertise (at least in areas that have not been politicized) when we take them to report the consensus in their field. When a journalist interviews an astronomer about what they hope we'll learn from the James Webb telescope, say, we rarely question or doubt the claims they make, so long as they confine themselves to their area of expertise. This is all completely rational. It is rational to assign higher credibility to experts; expertise just does confer epistemic credibility. Experts' assertions carry extra weight in virtue of the fact that they have more background knowledge and a much greater ability to assess claims within the domains of their expertise than laypeople.

If there's irrationality in the Einstein effect, it must be in virtue of the fact that the effect attaches to literally meaningless statements. It's one thing to attach high credibility to a doctor's diagnosis, or to the assertion from an astronomer that the Big Bang occurred 13.8 billion years ago, and quite another to assign high credibility to "Wholeness quiets infinite phenomena." In the first two cases, we assign a high credibility to an assertion we can parse for meaning; in the second, we assign high credibility to something that is entirely baffling. Surely *that's* irrational?

Again, I think this is a mistake. The assignment of credibility to an assertion shouldn't depend on our ability to understand it; not when it's a claim about a domain requiring special expertise. Consider two claims that are, for me, impenetrable but to which I assign high credibility:

$E = mc^2$
Quantum particles can be in a superposition of states that collapse into a single state on observation.

I assign these propositions a high degree of credibility because physicists take them to be credible, and they are propositions with regard to which physicists have epistemic privilege. Fundamental physics is, notoriously, a domain in which ordinary intuition is unreliable and any degree of understanding depends on painfully acquired esoteric knowledge. Given my lack of training in the domain, I should *expect* to find claims within it impenetrable. That shouldn't be a barrier to finding them credible. They're credible to me *because experts assert them*, not because I can assess them for myself, or even understand them.

You may well understand the propositions just mentioned better than I do. Still, you certainly accept *some* propositions you can't really clarify (whether you're aware that you can't clarify them or not; see Keil and Wilson [2000]; Rozenblit and Keil [2002] on the *illusion of explanatory depth*). Perhaps these propositions fall within the domain of physics or mathematics: perhaps (like me) you can't really clarify the claim that the universe consists of ten (or eleven) dimensions – again, a claim I assign some credence to. Perhaps they're propositions about biology: many more people accept the theory of evolution than are able to explain it, and even those with some undergraduate education in it are often seriously confused about it (Shtulman, 2006). We see the same phenomenon in the domain of religion. Think of notoriously opaque claims like "God is three in one." It's rational for (some) religious believers to accept claims like this (where this entails seeing them as credible and important), deferring to theologians and priests for their precise content.

The religious believer is rational in accepting such claims (given their background beliefs) for the same sort of reason I take myself to be rational in accepting the scientific claims I mentioned. We take these statements to be credible despite our inability to clarify them because we take them to concern issues that fall within a domain in which it takes genuine and deep expertise to have knowledge (or justified belief), and because we take these claims to be endorsed by those who possess the relevant expertise. Clarifiability doesn't enter into it: I have just as much – and just the same – reason to endorse the claims I can't clarify within such domains as those (if any) I *can* clarify. I do so on the basis of expert testimony, and my capacity to grasp the claims is irrelevant. Similarly, there's no particular reason to think that those who rate Deepak Chopra's tweets as credible and important are behaving irrationally in doing so, given *their* background beliefs.

The notion of rationality I'm invoking here is obviously subjectivist. To be rational, in the sense I have in mind, is a matter of updating one's attitudes on the evidence. It is not a matter of getting things right (though of course it's nonaccidentally connected to getting things right). Given bad evidence or bad background beliefs, someone may rationally update in a way that takes them further from the truth. Most readers will think that anyone who assigns high credibility to new age aphorisms has bad background beliefs. I agree; nevertheless *given* those beliefs, there's no reason to think they're updating badly. Those people who are subject to the Einstein effect may be subject to no rational defect at all: neither in endorsing the supposedly scientific claims nor in taking scientists to be domain experts.

Let's return to philosophy. Suppose (for the moment) that Balibar or Deleuze or Derrida (or Hegel or Wittgenstein or McDowell) deal in assertions that are "unclarifiable" for many (or even all) of their readers. Given the right set of background beliefs, it would nevertheless be rational to assign them a high degree of credibility and importance. Given the status of the philosopher in France, it is rational for the nonexpert to assign high credibility to such assertions when they are plausibly taken as falling within the domain of the speaker's expertise. There's nothing irrational about any of that.

1.3 Bullshit, Expert Level

This defense of French bullshit only takes us so far, however. I've argued that it's rational for nonexperts to assign high credibility to assertions they can't clarify, when they take those assertions to be endorsed by relevant experts. It follows that it might be rational for the average nonexpert to assign high credibility to the assertions of a philosopher. But it's one thing to show that it would be rational for the nonexpert to assign high credibility to an unclarifiable assertion and quite another to show that it would be rational for a *professional philosopher* to do the same. The philosopher is in the position of the physicist who reads a statement like "Turbulence is born in the gap where transformation has been excluded," attributed to another physicist. Unlike the layperson, they have the tools to assess it, and can appropriately call bullshit. Similarly, that it's rational for the nonexpert to assign high credibility to (say) Balibar's claims even though they're unclarifiable *for them* doesn't show that Gerry Cohen was making a mistake in calling bullshit.

Let's set Cohen himself aside for the moment. Before we discuss his justification for calling bullshit on Balibar, let's focus on more typical cases in which philosophers denigrate the work of other philosophers in these kinds of terms. Typically, these cases involve philosophers in one tradition denouncing work in another: say, the signatories of the infamous letter calling on the University of Cambridge not to award an honorary degree to Derrida (Smith, 1992). It is unlikely that Armstrong, Quine, or Ruth Barcan Marcus had much familiarity with Derrida's work. Their assessment of his work might have been based on casual acquaintance with it: reading excerpts or maybe an essay. Perhaps some of the signatories thought that intellectual responsibility required them to dip into Derrida in this kind of way before signing the letter. Perhaps some of them went deeper, reading several essays, a whole book, or even several books. Of course, there comes a point at which one has engaged sufficiently deeply with a philosopher to be in a good epistemic position to assess their work (one signatory of the letter, Kevin Mulligan, may have been in such a position). But it takes *serious* and *sustained* engagement to be in that position with regard to a philosopher working in a different tradition; more serious and sustained engagement than is commonly thought.

Science is highly specialized, and the expert chemist (say) may be at a loss when it comes to the claims of a physicist. With regard to claims like that, the chemist may be just as much a layperson as I am. They might assign high credibility to such claims for the same reasons I do. Philosophy is not (a) science, of course. But it is very diverse. Even *within* traditions, broadly conceived, there's a great deal of diversity: I struggle to understand work in much of the philosophy of science, for example. Across traditions there is a great deal more diversity, in subject matter, approach, and even stakes. I think it's plausible to maintain that those signatories to the Derrida letter who lacked serious acquaintance with his work were laypeople in Derrida's field. They simply lacked the expertise to make a serious attempt at clarifying his statements or otherwise assessing them.[4]

Genuine engagement with Derrida's work – say reading several of his books and even some commentary – is likely insufficient to acquire the expertise required to assess it, even for someone who is already an expert in a different philosophical tradition. At least on views I find plausible, genuine and *deep* immersion in a philosophical tradition is required. Philosophical traditions might constitute what Alasdair MacIntyre (1990) calls rival versions of inquiry, with incommensurable standards. Alternatively, and more weakly, they may not be incommensurable but they might have very different goals. If either of these views is true, Derrida's work might be bad philosophy *when it is assessed against the aims of paradigm analytic philosophy* but good philosophy when assessed against some other standard. Perhaps his claims about language don't illuminate its structure very well at all but succeed in bringing us to see the world anew, for example.

That's not to say that someone trained in a different tradition *can't* acquire the expertise justifiably to call bullshit on Derrida or some other philosopher. My training, up to and including PhD, was in continental philosophy, but I take myself to have acquired the expertise to assess some stretches of analytic philosophy (only *some* stretches: no one, or almost no one, is in a position to assess *all* of it, given how diverse and specialized it is). It is possible to acquire the expertise to make such assessments (note the opportunity-costs trap that looms here: it sometimes takes effort and work to discover whether it's worthwhile to make the effort to understand a thinker). There's also a much easier route to acquiring a justified belief that something is bullshit: testimony from someone who is genuinely expert in the relevant tradition. The degree to which

---

[4] Supposing, that is, that Derrida's assertions must be clarifiable, on pain of being bullshit. Cohen's clarifiability standard is question-begging: he notes that non-Western philosophers, who he doesn't regard as emitters of bullshit, sometimes didn't write, or attempt to write, in clarifiable assertions; we might think too of the pre-Socratics.

a belief acquired on the basis of such testimony is justified depends, *inter alia*, on the degree to which it reflects a consensus of those with expertise. It's not hard to find examples of people with impeccable credentials within the French poststructuralist tradition who dismiss Derrida's value (Foucault famously dismissed Derrida's "petty pedagogy" [Haddad, 2016]). If Foucault's testimony is heavily contested within his own tradition, though, we acquire the right to think nothing more definitive than *it is reasonable to believe that Derrida is bullshit* on its basis.

1.4 Clarifying the Unclarifiable

I've argued that most of us aren't justified in calling bullshit on the work of other philosophers, because we're rarely in a good epistemic position to make the call. But Cohen, surely, was in a good position to assess Balibar. He read, he tells us "a great deal" of Althusserian Marxism in his twenties (Cohen, 2013: 94), which surely positioned him to assess it. Further, it seems there are no grounds for worrying that he assessed it against an inappropriate standard: the aims of Althusserian Marxism are surely at least roughly the same aims as other work in the Marxist tradition. Cohen, at least, seems to have the right to call bullshit.[5] In principle, that's right: Cohen *does* have the right to call bullshit on Balibar. But even Cohen is on shaky ground here (for reasons that will be important when we – finally! – return to the discussion of peer review).

Recall Cohen's basis for calling bullshit: that Balibar's work is "unclarifiable." In defending this criterion of bullshit, Cohen is in good company (if not in Frankfurt's company); that's more or less how the empirical literature operationalizes "bullshit." Sterling, Jost, and Pennycook (2016), for example, characterize bullshit as "essentially meaningless." These assertions defeat all attempts, even the attempts of those with domain-relevant expertise, to clarify them. But is Balibar's work really unclarifiable?

Actually, I don't have much trouble clarifying the stimuli used in the experiments on bullshit, nor the extrusions of the new age sages. Take the paradigm of bullshit Pennycook *et al.* (2015: 549) cite as a central example: "Hidden meaning transforms unparalleled abstract beauty." That's not very hard to assign a content to. Meanings plainly can be hidden (perhaps this very aphorism is an example of such hidden meanings, though I don't think it's very well

---

[5] If we're required to conciliate in the face of peer disagreement, even an expert might not have the right to call bullshit on any thinker in the face of significant peer disagreement. I set this issue aside for the moment, noting only that any view on which peer disagreement rules out our capacity to call bullshit on other thinkers, no matter how deeply we're acquainted with their work, would raise a very serious problem of what has come to be called spinelessness (Fritz, 2018); that is, it would threaten very many of our beliefs in a way that seems intolerable.

hidden in this case). Such meanings could have a transformative effect on beauty, I suppose; that is, perhaps our perception of such beauty is quite different before and after grasping the hidden meaning. "Abstract beauty" might refer to the beauty of art that is not representational. It doesn't take a lot of work to assign a meaning to the assertion; it's sufficiently easy, I think, for it to be reasonable to believe that most people parse it as meaningful even on casual reading. I won't attempt it now, but I don't think it's all that difficult to assign a meaning to the Deepak Chopra tweet that Pennycook *et al.* cite as a paradigm of bullshit: "Attention and intention are the mechanics of manifestation."[6]

We need to look harder if we are to find examples of genuinely unclarifiable or "literally meaningless" statements to serve as stimuli for experiments. Perhaps we'll find them in the work of French philosophers, as Cohen thinks. Recall the "wonderful example" of bullshit he cites from Étienne Balibar: "This is precisely the first meaning we can give to the idea of dialectic: a logic or form of explanation specifically adapted to the determinant intervention of class struggle in the very fabric of history" (Balibar, 2014: 97). But is it *really* unclarifiable? Cohen's original discussion of bullshit came in response to Frankfurt and was published along with the latter's reply. Frankfurt offers what seems to me a straightforward and defensible interpretation of Balibar's assertion: "The most distinctive point of dialectical explanations is precisely that they are supposed to be particularly helpful in illuminating how class struggle has determined the course of history" (Frankfurt, 2002: 342).

Why does Frankfurt, who I suspect has no great background in Marxism (let alone in the Althusserians) succeed in clarifying Balibar when Cohen does not? I think the difference lies in the degree of intellectual charity with which Cohen (and those who dismiss new age aphorisms as meaningless) approach the assertions they dismiss. Given even a minimally charitable attitude to these statements, we can easily make sense of at least most of them.

I've argued that one (defensible) reason for attributing a significant degree of credibility and importance to an assertion we can't clarify is because we take it to be an assertion by an expert, speaking within the domain of their expertise. I now want to add that whether we succeed in clarifying an assertion is also sensitive to how much prior credibility we assign to it and its source. *Because* they're attributed to a new age sage (or because features of their content suggest such an attribution), those with a low opinion of such people read them through an uncharitable interpretive frame and find little meaning in them. Similarly,

---

[6] For what it's worth, Chopra himself has offered an interpretation of this assertion (Goldhill, 2017).

I bet that Cohen rejects Balibar as meaningless *because he's disillusioned with Althusserian Marxism*. He has things backward: he thinks he rejects Balibar because he's meaningless; rather, he finds Balibar meaningless because he now has such a low opinion of his work.

Of course, none of this would arise were Deepak Chopra's tweets or Balibar's assertions models of pellucid clarity. It takes work to paraphrase their claims; that's why intellectual charity can make such a difference to whether we find them meaningful. Assertions vary in their clarity, and it's plausible to think that new age sages (and perhaps even some philosophers) exploit polysemy to avoid commitment to testable predictions. But, as Cohen himself recognizes, polysemy can be a virtue in a text: it can "stimulate thought" (Cohen, 2002: 334), and a number of philosophers have shared the early Wittgenstein's belief that though all attempts to articulate genuinely profound truths must "run against the boundaries of language," attempts at such articulation in poetic form deserve our deep respect (Wittgenstein, 1965). There are legitimate arguments concerning when lack of clarity is a flaw in a particular text. But neither Balibar nor the new age sages are genuinely unclarifiable; not to a minimally charitable reader.[7] If Cohen finds Balibar unclarifiable, it's likely because he can no longer read Balibar's work with sufficient charity to assign determinate content to it.

2 Intellectual Charity in Everyday (Academic) Life

Interesting though (I hope) they are, these reflections might appear to have little to do with peer review. In this section, I'm going to argue for their relevance. I'm going to argue that just as differences in intellectual charity underlie differences in the disposition to attribute bullshit, so they routinely make smaller differences in the interpretation of papers – for example, during peer review. The difference between *rejection* and *revise and resubmit* is often a difference in how charitably we've been read. In both cases, the degree of intellectual charity we extend to a text is a response (at least in part) to intra- and extratextual cues: cues that suggest who the author is, what other people have thought of the text, even (as we'll see in the last section of this Element) cues that suggest what attitude the author takes to their own arguments.

Here's a truism: arguments stand or fall on their own merits, regardless of who makes them. An argument's rational persuasiveness – the degree to which it *ought to* move us – is entirely independent of who makes it, in what context,

---

[7] It's *hard* to construct a "literally meaningless" statement. Chomsky's famous attempt – "colorless green ideas sleep furiously" – deliberately combines predicates that conflict: "colorless" and "green," most obviously. But if we're disposed to read the sentence allusively, we can extract some sort of sense from it (see the Wikipedia page on the sentence for a number of attempts to assign it some sort of meaning; ("*Colorless Green Ideas Sleep Furiously*", 2022).

and how it is framed. Ideally, we can capture its true strength by formalizing it in sentential logic. This truism, like most truisms I suspect, is far from entirely true: how persuasive we ought to find an argument *isn't* independent of who makes it. How much we trust the source can make a decisive difference (Dutilh Novaes, 2020). I suggest that making such a difference is rationally defensible.

Every text admits of multiple interpretations, some more consistent and more coherent than others. That fact ensures we must make interpretive decisions: do we read it in an attempt to make it consistent (which might require us occasionally to dismiss some statements as slips by the author), or are we on the lookout for inconsistencies and howlers? Of course, the text must strongly constrain our interpretation. I'm not suggesting anything goes, and no matter how charitably we read them, some texts just can't justifiably be given a consistent and plausible interpretation. But all texts of any complexity and ambition take interpretive work to make sense of, and all require us to make (often implicit) interpretive decisions. How charitable we are in reading affects what interpretive decisions we make.

When we read our peers, say in the context of reviewing their work for a journal, we rarely set out to read uncharitably, and we almost never read so uncharitably as to struggle to see meaning in their work. But intellectual charity comes in degrees. The continuum of charity is indefinitely gradable: between the extremes of zero charity and maximal charity we may occupy any position.

A high degree of intellectual charity is often explicitly called for in approaching the work of the dead greats. Bennett (1982: 755) sets out the principle of charity widely held to govern appropriate interpretation of such thinkers as follows:

> "We should make the philosopher under study true where we can, and otherwise reasonable, subject to the condition that our account of him [sic] not be slippery, evasive about difficulties or based on special pleadings, and to the further condition that we don't purchase truth for him at the expense of making him tame or boring."

On this Quinean construal of the principle, we ought to interpret the words of the dead greats so as to maximize the number of truths – by our lights – their texts contain. Such a principle risks anachronism. Worse, it prevents us from engaging with minds that are to some degree alien to ours and thereby forestalls the challenges to our common sense that the thinking of the distant (in time and in space) might provide us with. As Melamed (2013) says, it *domesticates* the thinking of others. Especially when we're engaging with work from different cultures, this isn't a principle we should adopt. Instead, we should adopt the principle advocated by Campbell (to whom Bennett is replying): rather than interpret the dead greats as *correct* (by our lights), we should see them as arguing well. As Campbell puts it, "obscurity and self-contradiction" in the texts of the greats should be seen as "*prima facie* evidence of misinterpretation" (Campbell, 1980: 585).[8]

A high level of intellectual charity of this kind is supposedly justified in relation to the dead greats because they *are* greats.[9] We should be intellectually humble in the face of their work, assuming that their arguments are powerful and – in the light of *their* presuppositions – plausible, even if we have trouble grasping their points. Such a degree of charity would be out of place when reading lesser mortals: the confusions or obscurities we think we see are more likely genuinely to be there in, say, my work. We approach journal reviewing with a moderate (or lower) degree of charity, and a greater willingness to attribute confusion or error, because we assume the author is a mere mortal, like us, and not one of the greats. Given signs of scholarly competence, we adopt a much higher degree of intellectual charity than the minimal level with which we read Deepak Chopra. We adjust our intellectual charity up or down in response to all sorts of (intratextual) cues as we go. We're likely to be more charitable to a paper that is well-written, for instance (perhaps at the risk of epistemic injustice to non-native speakers), to those that cite the contemporary literature, and so on. These differences in the degree of charity with which we read can make a big difference to our overall assessment of texts.

Thanks to the ways in which intra- and extratextual cues affect interpretation, arguments (typically) *don't* stand on their own merits, regardless of how they're expressed and who expresses them. An argument from someone we trust is more persuasive than the same argument would be from someone we don't trust. It's uncontroversial, after all, that trust is essential for the transmission of knowledge via testimony, and arguments rely on testimony, as well as on inference. At minimum, they often have premises which are transmitted via testimony, and which therefore must be taken on trust. Most arguments call upon our trust in assessing their cogency too: relations of support between premises are often not always clear and perspicuous (whether due to the limitations of the source, the recipient, or the difficulty of the material itself);

---

[8] Contra Malamed, *some* degree of Quineanism is justified in interpreting those we regard with reverence. We should avoid attributing error by our *shared* lights, and by the lights of their culture, unless there is a strong reason to do so.

[9] Are they? I suspect that the riches we find in them owe a great deal to their history of interpretation and to the charity with which we approach them, and that other texts could have played the same role in the canon (I'll have more to say on how the reception of a text can affect its value in a few moments). Canonical works probably need to pass a high bar to play the role they do, but chance (and prejudice) no doubt plays a large role in which of the many candidates for canonization come to be included within the canon.

evidential support can be a matter of degree, and the more we trust the arguer, the more strongly we may – justifiably – take the premises to support the conclusion (Dutilh Novaes, 2020).

When we trust the author, we extend greater intellectual charity, and with good reason: the greater our intellectual trust in the author, the more we come to the text believing that reading it is a worthwhile use of our time, and the more willing we are to attribute difficulties and confusions to ourselves, rather than the text. How we interpret the text and how persuasive we find it will depend very significantly on how charitably we read it. Every argument has gaps: whether we see them as fatal flaws (warranting a reject verdict), problems that need addressing (revise and resubmit), or simply as issues rightly set aside in the name of pursuing other goals (accept!) may depend on how charitably we read the paper. We may see a lack of clarity as evidence the author is not thinking hard enough, or as inevitable given the difficulty of the material (perhaps some topics require us to run up to, or near, the boundaries of language). We may regard the assumptions made as reasonable in the context, or as begging crucial questions. These differences help settle how we respond.

All of this is rationally defensible. First, it reflects the need to allocate our scarce resources, of time and attention, intelligently. We can't pore over every paper with the attention we might devote to a particularly difficult passage in Hegel, hoping to uncover the wisdom we're confident is there. Second and more directly, though, it reflects an allocation of trust that is itself rationally defensible. The higher our opinion of the author and the work, the more charity we should invest in reading the text and the harder we should work to explain away apparent inconsistencies and unclarities. How much effort we put into interpreting a claim reflects our prior assessment of how worthwhile it is. Maximal intellectual charity is rightly reserved for the greats: we should be far readier to find confusion and triviality in one another.

2.1 Reading the Journals

Let's apply these insights to contemporary journals, via a case study of sorts. Jason Stanley is a major contemporary philosopher. Much of the recent attention to his work has focused on his books on propaganda (Stanley, 2015) and fascism (Stanley, 2018), but he was a central figure in philosophy well before he began to publish on these kinds of issues. In particular, his monograph on epistemology (Stanley, 2005) has been very influential. Writing on Facebook, Stanley noted an oddity about the reception of that book. It was, at the time of writing, the fifth most cited work since 2000 in the four most prestigious journals in philosophy: *Philosophical Review*, *Mind*, *Noûs*, and the *Journal of*

Philosophy. But the book itself had developed out of a paper rejected by three of these four journals. "All of those journals have accepted papers discussing, in many cases very centrally, a work those very journals have deemed unpublishable" (Stanley, quoted in Dutilh Novaes, 2013).

Catarina Dutilh Novaes, whose work on the role of trust in argumentation I've drawn on here, takes this tale to suggest that peer review doesn't do a good job of tracking quality (see also Arvan, Bright, and Heesen [2022]). While no system is immune to error, at least one of these journals should have identified Stanley's work as demanding publication – shouldn't they? I'm unconvinced that this case – or indeed, multiple such cases – provides much evidence in favor of the view that peer review is broken. Even setting aside obvious concerns (perhaps journal feedback, and the passing of time, allowed Stanley to improve the work), there are good reasons to think more highly of Stanley's work *after* it was published than of the same work when it was submitted to journals. Reading it now, we have intratextual and (especially) extratextual evidence of its quality that was unavailable to reviewers (much of it unavailable in principle, and therefore unavailable to assessors in any replacement for peer review). This evidence makes a justifiable difference to how we assess the quality of the work. Some of it provides guidance with regard to the value the text possessed all along. More radically, some of it may help to *constitute* that value.

2.1.1 Context as Higher-Order Evidence

An argument might be defined as the presentation of evidence in order to convince the receiver that something is the case. The evidence we focus on when we think about arguments is almost always the *first-order* evidence, the evidence that directly bears on whether p. We might think of the sources cited to establish premises, or the thought experiments designed to prompt intuitions, or the experimental data presented. Or we might focus on the formal structure of the argument: Is it deductively valid? Do the sources genuinely support the conclusion? And so on. But arguments also come bundled with *higher-order* evidence. For example, the extended argument that is a journal article often comes packaged with graphs or equations. The content of these graphs and equations is first-order evidence, but as Dan Sperber (2010) notes, the apparatus is itself evidence independent of its content: not evidence that p, but evidence that there is evidence for p. *Prior* to (and even independent of) whether one examines the graph or the equation, recognition of the fact that the argument is accompanied by this kind of formal apparatus is evidence in its favor. Of course, unscrupulous people can and do take advantage of this fact to give their arguments an unearned weight (American conspiracy theorist Glenn Beck is well-known for buttressing his arguments with diagrams drawn on a chalkboard to give them a spurious appearance of rigor). As Sperber notes, however, it's rational to increase one's credence in arguments in the light of such higher-order evidence: even if one can't assess an equation for oneself, the fact that the person has gone to the trouble of setting out their argument so carefully, in a way that exposes it to refutation by those with the appropriate expertise, is evidence that they themselves possess expertise and that they believe the argument will survive expert scrutiny, and both are evidence in favor of the argument. Evidence can be misleading and still be evidence.

This sort of intratextual evidence is available to reviewers and subsequent readers alike. But acceptance by a journal leads to the generation of further intra- and extratextual evidence. That *this paper was accepted by a (highly selective) journal* is itself higher-order evidence for its value. This fact ensures that readers are now in a very different epistemic position in relation to the paper than the reviewers were: they have different sets of evidence available to them. It follows that some of the evidence cited for the claim that peer review is broken is undercut. The fact that *three high-profile journals rejected work that subsequently appeared in an influential and important book* is at best weak evidence that these journals aren't tracking quality (or even that on these occasions they failed to track quality), because the reviewers did not have the same evidence available to them as we do, looking back.

A submission to *Mind* stands on its own: it owes whatever power it has to persuade (and, somewhat independently, to make its case for publication) to intratextual evidence, especially (but not only) the first-order evidence it presents. Reviewers have only this evidence to go on. Editors have a little more, assuming the journal does not practice triple anonymous review (*Mind* was actually one of the few journals to have such a policy when Stanley submitted his paper): knowing the identity of the author provides them with higher-order evidence for (or against!) the paper's reliability. But even editors have little beyond the paper itself to go on. An accepted paper, or a published book, presents a different and larger set of evidence.

The fact that *this paper was accepted by Mind* is evidence that the paper is worthwhile: that the argument is compelling or at any rate interesting and that the topic is a worthwhile one. More strongly, it provides evidence that the paper is of a quality higher than the many – the large majority – that were rejected by *Mind*. It *might* also be evidence that this paper is of a higher quality than the many published by (supposedly) lesser journals. After all, it's widely believed that *Mind* reviewers apply especially rigorous standards and are especially expert in their fields; whether you believe this or not, publication in *Mind* is evidence that the paper has survived a quality filtering process that most fail, and that's evidence in favor of its value.

It may be that as a matter of fact *Mind* doesn't filter papers for quality much better than less prestigious journals. There's some evidence that prestige doesn't correlate with quality in other fields (Heesen and Bright, 2020). It's definitely true that selection processes are shot through with arbitrariness, and I'm confident that, in terms of quality, there's nothing to distinguish accepted papers from the hundreds of near misses. Still, acceptance at *Mind* is higher-order evidence that supports thinking the paper is better than most submitted to any decent philosophy journal. Most are *not* near misses. A large chunk are not especially interesting or especially strong. A few are barely competent. An accepted paper has sufficiently convinced at least two reviewers and at least one editor that it deserves publication. It's very likely to be better than most (though far from all) the papers that were rejected. In any case, being accepted is evidence of its quality, whether it's *strong* evidence or not.

2.1.2 Reception as Higher-Order Evidence

Of course, publication is only the beginning of a paper's postacceptance life. Some papers go on to be widely cited and discussed. A few go on to spark entire new subfields. Think of the impact that "The Extended Mind" (Clark and Chalmers, 1998) had in helping to spawn a whole area of interdisciplinary inquiry. "The Extended Mind" was itself a paper that was rejected multiple times by multiple journals (Schliesser, 2013). Its impact attests to the qualities of the paper. It is very unlikely that another paper selected at random from among the many that were rejected would have had anything like that impact. After all, most *accepted* papers have little impact.

The postpublication history of a paper provides two sorts of evidence for its value. First, it provides evidence about its *intrinsic* quality: that history helps to reveal what the evidence supported all along. As Hedden (2019) argues, the way that events turn out provides us with evidence about the strength and direction of the evidence we possessed beforehand. That's why hindsight bias is not a bias, Hedden claims: that some event we had not predicted occurred is genuinely evidence that the facts prevailing prior to the occurrence provided evidence *for* that occurrence. Most papers don't make points that are sufficiently important and novel to demand citation by subsequent work in philosophy (a low citation discipline; Schwitzgebel, 2022). Very, very few are sufficiently groundbreaking to spark new subfields. So the reception history of a paper helps to reveal qualities that were already there, prior to its publication. Reception history provides higher-order evidence in favor of a paper's qualities, constituting evidence that was not available to reviewers. In addition, however, reception history can help to *constitute* the (relational) quality of the paper.

That *a paper is widely discussed*, or is *central to a subfield*, or has *sparked a whole cottage industry*, are facts about the paper that supervene on its reception. Even when this reception history reveals merits the paper genuinely possessed from the start, it's overwhelmingly likely that there was no inevitability that it had the effect it did. Was it inevitable that epistemology came to be obsessed with the role of epistemic luck in the way it did after Gettier's little paper (apparently) showing that a true justified belief may not always count as knowledge (Gettier, 1963)? Was it inevitable that debates over moral responsibility came to be obsessed with the attitudes of attributers in the way it did after Strawson's paper on the topic (Strawson, 1962)? I doubt it. I'm not doubting the fruitfulness of these approaches. I'm suggesting that debates could easily have gone in different directions, possibly with other papers playing an equally fruitful, though very different, role. As it happens, though, those other papers – which were arguably just as excellent and just as full of potential as the papers that displaced them – instead languished in obscurity.

Subsequent debates do not reveal that the texts that sparked them were better all along than the many that might have played analogous roles. They reflect, rather, the fact that they happened to be taken up. But for some chance events (say, a prominent philosopher happened to write a response, when they might easily have chosen to spend their time on something else), the debate might never have taken off. It might be the debate itself, and not the paper that sparked it, that is the locus of real value, and there might be no special reason to expect *that* paper to have sparked the debate. In actual cases, it's likely impossible to disentangle the intrinsic merits of a paper from its role in a debate. Its subsequent fruitfulness alters the degree of intellectual charity with which we read it, and thereby our perception of its merits. It might even partly constitute those merits.

2.2 Back to the Case Study

Knowledge and Practical Interests (Stanley, 2005) is a book, not a journal article. But it's a book from Oxford University Press (OUP), widely regarded as the most prestigious publisher in academic philosophy (Leiter, 2013). Indeed, it's a book from the Clarendon Press of OUP; the "Clarendon Press" imprint was, at the time when Stanley's book was published, given to titles the press regarded as "of particular academic importance" (Oxford University Press, 2009). It is, moreover, a book by Jason Stanley, a major figure in contemporary philosophy (even if Stanley's reputation rests, in important part, on *Knowledge and Practical Interests*, that reputation can appropriately affect our perception of the book). Finally, it's a book that has received a great deal of discussion. It's been cited more than 1,600 times and papers that discuss it in depth have been published in major journals.[10] All of this constitutes strong higher-order evidence in favor of its value (and might even help to constitute its merits) – evidence that was not available to reviewers and editors when Stanley's paper was submitted to the journals.

Confession time: I haven't read *Knowledge and Practical Interests*. But I'm very confident that it's an excellent book. Publication by OUP would be enough for me to think it's worthwhile. I have sufficient faith in the press, its commissioning editors, and its reviewers to be confident that the books the press publishes are usually significant contributions to philosophy. The fact that it's by Jason Stanley is further evidence that convinces me of its quality. As a matter of fact, I have read some of Stanley's work carefully (see Levy 2017 for discussion of his work on knowledge how), but I would be confident in its quality even if I had never read him. Too many of my peers (and, in this domain, epistemic superiors) think highly of him for me to doubt his quality. His professorship at Yale is also higher-order evidence of his quality, largely because occupying a position like that is *third*-order evidence: it's evidence that his peers think highly of him because such a reputation is needed to be appointed to such a position. It's also evidence he has an excellent publication record, and that's further evidence of his quality.

All this evidence – evidence about the book and its influence, and about Stanley – convinces me that *Knowledge and Practical Interests* is excellent.[11] None of it, or almost none of it, was available to the reviewers of the paper that became the book (most of it couldn't be available to them, since it didn't yet exist, of course). They had much less to go on. So the puzzle Stanley points to – why would a book merit serious discussion in the pages of leading journals, when the paper which formed its core didn't merit publication in these journals? – really isn't so mysterious. A central part of the answer is that reviewers for the journals didn't then have the evidence that now supports an especially high appraisal of the work.

---

[10] Note the potential here for snowball effects: the more attention a book receives, the more evidence there is that it deserves attention.

[11] A reviewer of this Element notes two worries here. First, they note that if I was asked my opinion of Stanley's book, it would be misleading for me to say "it's excellent!" without qualification. It would be misleading because such an answer implicates that I'd read it. I think that's right, but it reflects facts about pragmatics, not the evidential value of my testimony. I suspect our preference for first-order evidence that underlies the pragmatics here is in fact unjustified. Second, the reviewer worries about double-counting: if Stanley got his professorship at Yale on the basis of the book, that professorship doesn't provide *additional* evidence for the book's quality. This is a conclusion I want to resist. While the amount of additional evidence every further honor or publication provides rapidly diminishes, they may each rationally be taken as providing some further evidence about the quality of the book itself. Consideration for honors is a filter, and passing through the filter adds some further evidence of quality.

Let's spend a little more time on this claim, because the position I'm arguing for is counterintuitive. Of course, most people accept that the kind of factors I've pointed to – the prestige of the author, of their academic appointment, their citations, and so on – *influence* reviewers and editors. There's little controversy about that. But the consensus view is that this represents an obstacle to epistemically fair assessment of work; indeed, an epistemic injustice. It's *prestige bias*: the same bias that leads hiring committees to prefer candidates from "better" schools to equally (or even better) qualified candidates from schools that are less well thought of (De Cruz, 2018). Mentioning the prestige of Stanley and his book may *explain* why his work is now widely discussed when it was once rejected, but it doesn't go any way toward *justifying* it.

I'm suggesting, in contrast, that prestige is often genuine evidence: that is, it provides considerations that justify changing beliefs. It's evidence on both a subjectivist and a more objective account of evidence. On a subjectivist account, a fact or proposition is evidence for you if it's (really) the case that you ought to adjust your beliefs upon learning it, *given your prior beliefs*.[12] Of course, this subjectivist account of evidence accommodates pernicious biases: for someone with prejudiced beliefs, a person's gender could be evidence of inferiority, for example. On a subjectivist account, evidence need not be objectively *good* evidence. Prestige is clearly often genuine evidence in *this* sense: it's uncontroversial that people do take the prestige of an author or a book to be a reason to think well of it, compared to how they would assess the same arguments presented in the absence of this higher-order evidence. So, too, is the prestige of the institution from which someone graduated genuine evidence for the assessor, if this person believes that institutional reputation is a reliable predictor of candidate quality.[13]

It is (subjectively) rational for agents to update their beliefs on their evidence (Levy, 2021). Agents who update like this are functioning well, in one important respect: their internal systems are working as designed. The person for whom p is evidence, given their background beliefs, might have bad background

---

[12] Or if it's the case that you would be required to adjust your beliefs upon learning it, had you not already taken it into account, perhaps indirectly, or were it not defeated or trumped by some other evidence.

[13] In philosophy, most reviewing is double anonymous – reviewers don't know the identity of the author and the author doesn't know the identity of the reviewers – and occasionally triple anonymous, with author identity hidden from editors too. In many other disciplines, peer review is only single anonymous: reviewers know the identity of the author. There's a lively debate over the value of single versus double (or triple) anonymous review, and the higher-order evidence that author identity provides is often cited in justification of the former: defenders of single anonymity argue that only in the light of the track record of the author, and even in the light of consideration of the institution that employs them, can papers be fairly assessed (Pontille and Torny 2014; Palus 2015; see Rowbottom 2022 for further discussion).

beliefs but updating on *p* is rational for them. In addition, though, markers of prestige may often be *objectively good* evidence: genuine indicators of quality. Exactly when prestige is genuinely good evidence is of course an empirical question: it must be the case that the markers of prestige correlate sufficiently reliably with the properties they're taken to be evidence for. Although there's no doubt that it influences us when it shouldn't, prestige often does correlate with these kinds of properties.

Outside philosophy, employers often prefer graduates from "good" schools to those from less prestigious institutions. I think we're right to be troubled by this, but *not* because this preference isn't rational. Talent may be evenly distributed at birth (or perhaps there's no reasonable way of cashing out talk of talent and potential at birth), but it's not the case that as adults, people are still equally able. What's really troubling isn't that jobs go to the privileged regardless of their ability (though that does happen) but that ability itself is unfairly distributed. Birth plays a big role in who becomes talented. Encouragement, exposure to a variety of stimuli, reward for achievement, and so on; these things make an enormous difference to people's capacities. We should expect those who graduate from Harvard to be more articulate and confident and in many domains (including those that employers, rightly or wrongly, value) more able than those who went to less prestigious schools. Even if a Harvard education is no better than that available elsewhere, Harvard students should be expected to be better than most: Harvard is able to choose from those who've stood out, and those from privileged backgrounds are more likely to stand out.[14]

The degree to which prestige correlates with quality is surely lower than it ought to be: many things that are not valuable influence the attribution of prestige. Indeed, prestige has plausibly come to be weaponized in philosophy. For example, the prestige ranking of subfields was established by people who lacked genuine acquaintance with the areas of philosophy they dismiss (or even testimony from those with such acquaintance); unsurprisingly, it's a very unreliable cue to quality. This unjustified prestige hierarchy contributes to the dismissal of wide swathes of philosophy as bullshit. This hierarchy interacts with other illegitimate markers of prestige, such as accent or even simply what Bourdieu (1998) called "cultural capital," such as an easy familiarity with wine and books (think of the examples that populate many philosophical papers and how they convey social status). It may often or even always be *unjust* to treat prestige as evidence, because prestige reflects undeserved background conditions. In these cases, it is also *unjustified*. It compounds disadvantage and leaves

---

[14] Why is this unjust? One reason is because it ensures that rewards tend to flow upwards to those who need them least. It's unsurprising that social mobility is low, when the very characteristics that meritocracy rewards are distributed on the basis of income and class.

those who want to pursue other questions and other approaches facing a demand to legitimate themselves as worthwhile (Dotson, 2013).

We can make prestige more reliable and fight its weaponization by recognizing that prestige is most reliable when it is *local* (because expertise is local). For a variety of reasons (from pernicious influences, like the effects of insider networks, through to gaps in the expertise of editors and the lower rates at which women submit to more prestigious journals [Krishnamurthy *et al.*, 2017; Wilhelm, Conklin, and Hassoun, 2018]), the best work in many fields does not tend to appear in the most prestigious journals. Publication in the most prestigious journals should itself be seen as evidence of *local* excellence: excellence in the domains they focus on. Local cues to prestige must align with local criteria for excellence: As Dotson (2013: 18) urges, the inappropriate demand for legitimation should be met not only with a proliferation of different kinds of philosophy, but equally a proliferation of "canonical works and criteria that will be used as justifying norms." Such a proliferation will entail a proliferation of (local) extratextual cues to quality and a more appropriate alignment of prestige with excellence.

It's also true that even within domains in which they're relevant, cues to prestige may be used inappropriately. In many cases, such cues should be screened off by better information. *That someone went to Harvard* is an indicator of their ability, but a later record of failure suggests that the indicator is an unreliable one. In hiring in philosophy, later achievement routinely screens off earlier evidence. *That someone has a PhD from Cornell* is evidence of quality, but later publications should screen it off, because it provides stronger evidence for the same qualities. Other things being equal, we should prefer the better published Shelbyville College graduate over the worse published Cornell PhD. In fact, given the advantages that accrued to the latter, and the obstacles faced by the former, it's arguably rational to prefer an equally well-published Shelbyville grad to the Cornell PhD: their record is evidence they're *better* than their competitor, since they had to overcome more obstacles and make their own way without the guidance of a well-placed network. Similar considerations apply to admission to grad school: letters from prestigious individuals (say) constitute genuine evidence, but also reflect advantages (networking opportunities, for example) that others may not have had, and responses should be adjusted in that light.

Either way, a record of excellent publications is genuine evidence of excellence. To be sure, it's not evidence of excellence alone: it *also* reflects unmerited advantage. If you have an excellent record of publication, that's probably (in important part) because your job is less demanding than many. You don't have a 5/5 teaching load, you're not a freeway flier, patching together a living across multiple campuses; your home life is supportive rather than draining; you have access to resources and time to reflect. These are close to necessary conditions of excellence in publication (I'm aware of exceptions, but they're rare – and all the more impressive for overcoming these obstacles). Excellence has undeserved background and causal conditions; that doesn't entail it's not excellence. If you're selecting between candidates one of whom has manifested such excellence and one who has not, you'd be taking a gamble to prefer the second: perhaps they're capable of work every bit as good or better, but in many circumstances you're not entitled to believe that's likely. Higher-order evidence is often objectively good evidence, and in some contexts markers of prestige fit this model.

Assessing the actual evidential weight of (say) a PhD from a prestigious school versus a PhD from a less prestigious one is obviously a difficult exercise; one made all the more difficult by the fact that evidential weight is context-dependent and comparative: it is always evidence, but its strength depends on what other facts obtain. Fortunately, making these judgments are not required for my project. I need only to show that prestigious publication and pedigree *is* evidence. It's evidence we ought to take into account in assessing the quality of philosophical work.

Although excellence is found well beyond the most prestigious journals, and though publication in prestigious journals reflects many factors, some pernicious, publication in these journals is genuine evidence of excellence. Equally, publication by a prestigious press is genuine evidence of excellence. It's the latter evidence which explains the different epistemic positions of contemporary readers of *Knowledge and Practical Interests* and the reviewers who rejected Stanley's paper. Those reviewers took the paper seriously, as they were rationally bound to, on the basis of the strength of the arguments it presented them with (of course this sort of first-order evidence strongly constrains rational response). They saw it as serious and worthwhile philosophy – the original paper received no fewer than three revise and resubmits from *Philosophical Review*, which all by itself is higher-order evidence of its quality. But differences in intellectual charity may justifiably make the difference between seeing a paper as one among many high-quality submissions to the journal and one that is really compelling.

The reviewers, or the editors, saw it as excellent, but as not quite excellent, or not quite exciting, enough. Were they making a mistake? Was Stanley's work so excellent that it *demanded* acceptance (where a text demands acceptance when it is an objective mistake to prefer to publish other excellent work rather than it)? Perhaps it was, but if it was, it was very much the exception among the work that is submitted, and even among that actually published. While lots of work in philosophy is merely good, there's more excellent work than there are slots in the high-profile journals. Little of that excellent work stands out as genuinely *demanding* acceptance.

Much (most?) of the work submitted to philosophy journals is worthwhile: it is competently written and argued, and makes a genuine contribution to the philosophical literature. But editors and reviewers are looking for more. The current system is *designed* to have fewer slots than good papers: it's supposed to act as a filter through which only significantly-better-than-merely-good papers pass.[15] The criteria for competence are probably easier to apply than the criteria for excellence. To judge whether a paper is competent, I need to assess whether the arguments are cogent, whether it is written comprehensibly, whether it cites a sufficiently broad range of relevant literature, whether it interprets the work of others defensibly, and whether the point it is making is at least minimally novel or underappreciated. No doubt there's room for reasonable disagreement on these questions, but there's much less room for such disagreement on them than on whether the paper is significantly better than competent. The current invitation to review for *Mind* asks reviewers to note that the editors "are looking for papers of significant interest that are not merely small contributions to an existing discussion." We have no algorithm for assessing when a paper passes that bar, and none for trading off the various other criteria that papers are rightly judged against. Suppose we're satisfied the paper is of 'significant interest': how do we weigh that against the perceived holes in the argument? There are many papers that are, in one way or another, excellent and there's plenty of room for reasonable disagreement about which of them deserve publication.[16]

---

[15] Perhaps we should reject the current system in favor of one that allows many more papers to be published, such that no excellent (or even, perhaps, no merely good) paper is rejected. There are many models we might pursue. Heesen and Bright (2020) advocate a system whereby researchers upload their papers to an online repository when they judge them ready for distribution, with little or no gatekeeping; on their model, peer review would be postpublication and journals would publish a curated selection of such articles (see Rowbottom [2022] for an argument that this proposal would have epistemic costs). Other philosophers have advocated a less radical overhaul: noting that journal space is no longer limited by printing costs, they've suggested significantly increasing the number of papers accepted. I won't comment on these proposals, except to note that they're unlikely to achieve what some (but only some) of their advocates want: broader distribution of recognition. They leave in place mechanisms (like postpublication review) that filter work, making some of it salient and leaving much neglected. In many cases, philosophers who advocate increasing the number of papers published seem to aim to achieve the prestige of publication in a highly selective journal by way of making journals less selective. That's not something they can have, even if they're right that their rejected paper was just as worthwhile as some that were accepted.

[16] Arvan, Bright, and Heesen (2022) presuppose that there is a fact of the matter concerning the relative quality of papers. While it is possible to sort papers into quality bands, I doubt there's any fine-grained objective ranking. It is therefore harder than they appreciate to assess the success of reviewers at identifying relative quality.

I don't know whether Stanley's paper *demanded* publication. But I'm confident that most of the papers published in excellent journals are not better than many that didn't make it. Rather, the authors were luckier: reviewers just happened to think better of their paper than another, due to idiosyncratic (but defensible) preferences and no doubt often due to sheer chance (the paper looked good in contrast to the last one the reviewer read; they happened to be in the right mood; they happened to be thinking about that issue just yesterday). There are (by design) fewer slots in journals than there are excellent papers, and it is partly a matter of luck which of these excellent papers makes it through. I'm confident that *none* of my papers demanded publication: had the editors decided to reject those they accepted, they wouldn't have been making any kind of rational error (conversely, some they rejected could have been accepted without anyone having a right to complain).

Being accepted by *Mind* (say) is evidence of excellence, but also partially a matter of luck. It is therefore partially a matter of luck which papers come to accrete the extratextual higher-order evidence that attests to their excellence: citations, responses, and so on. The fact that a paper is subsequently discussed is not evidence that it demanded acceptance, nor is it evidence that rejection by another journal was a mistake. Even when the evidence that subsequently accrues is rightly taken as indicating merits that make the paper genuinely outstanding and not merely excellent, it would be a mistake to convict the reviewers of error on the basis of this evidence: after all, it wasn't available to them, and they can't be faulted for failing to take it into account. Perhaps the paper I am reviewing right now for *The Journal of Good Ideas* will – or would – prove especially fruitful for subsequent debates, but that this is so is most clearly shown by its *actually* proving fruitful. Subsequent history both attests to the genuine qualities of the paper, *and* reflects luck in its uptake. It's near impossible to disentangle the relative contribution of luck and quality in its subsequent history: we can only say of Stanley's submission that it (like many other rejected and accepted papers, no doubt) was good enough to be fruitful in the way it has been.[17]

A big part of the reason why Cohen found Balibar's work to be bullshit is that he approached it with little intellectual charity. Much the same can be said for

---

[17] Peters and Ceci (1982) resubmitted papers that had already been accepted by prestigious journals in psychology to the very same journals, with only the names of the authors and their institutional affiliation changed (these were all journals using single anonymous review). Eight out of the nine that went to peer review were rejected, usually on the basis of methodological flaws (the ones that didn't go to peer review were recognized as duplicates of already accepted articles). Gans and Shepherd (1994) repeated the experiment with articles by leading economists, including Nobel Prize winners, with similar results. I don't see any reason to be surprised by these findings, or to think they indicate a serious problem with peer review.

(many of) those who dismiss Derrida's work as bullshit: at the very least, were they more charitable they would find something of interest in his work or concede that it might be worthwhile for other people engaged in other kinds of projects. But the attitude we take to a text can make much smaller differences: as well as making the difference between bullshit and the clarifiable, it can make the difference between the good and the excellent. It can also make the difference between "reject" and "revise and resubmit": the difference in verdict can reflect how much trust in the author the reviewer was disposed to feel. Intellectual charity can be cashed out as a kind of trust: a trust that the work is coherent, consistent, and significant. It's because (for some more or less idiosyncratic reason) they invested more trust in my paper that reviewers recommended it be accepted, rather than some other, equally deserving, paper.

Intellectual charity is, plausibly enough, an epistemic virtue, so perhaps we might reasonably demand that reviewers for journals approach every paper charitably. Many of those who dismiss Derrida as a charlatan may in fact be violating an intellectual obligation. But the suggestion that we owe every paper intellectual charity leaves it open how *much* charity we should extend. We shouldn't read every submission with the trust in the author we extend to a dead great: we shouldn't assume that apparent inconsistencies and flaws always reflect our limitations and not those of the text. Charity is indefinitely gradable, and there's such a thing as being too charitable. Some texts really are inconsistent; some arguments really are badly flawed, and some papers should be rejected. We can only judge, as best we can, how much charity to extend.

Our assessment of work in philosophy, and no doubt in other disciplines too, is sensitive to the degree of intellectual charity we extend, but there's no algorithm for settling how much is sufficient and how much is excessive. How much intellectual charity we extend is settled by all sorts of things, including how well-written the article is, our personal preferences in philosophy, and even our passing moods. Is it unjust that *your* paper was rejected when another was accepted? Arguably it is: your paper may have been every bit as deserving. We need to recognize that philosophy – like every other academic discipline – doesn't hand out goods to all and only the deserving. When it works well (and frequently it doesn't) it selects more or less randomly from among the many who are good enough. Those who are rewarded are always lucky, and the unrewarded are very often unlucky. We should work to eliminate the many bad kinds of pernicious bias that persist in philosophy, and also the cult of genius that confuses luck with merit. We should also work to explore alternative ways of recognizing quality: perhaps there are fairer methods. I'm skeptical, though, that we can eliminate the effects of intellectual charity on who is rewarded and who is not.

3 Too Much Trust? The Lesson of Hoaxes

In the previous section, I applied lessons learned about the effects of intellectual charity, and about the intra- and extratextual cues that modulate it, to peer review. I argued that attention to these cues undercuts some of the supposed evidence for the unreliability of peer review. A reviewer and the subsequent reader have different sets of evidence available to them, and reviewers cannot be accused of error in failing to be guided by evidence that did not yet exist. In this section and in Section 4, I move to somewhat different issues that arise in peer review, considered broadly. The first, to be discussed in this section, concerns whether reviewers ought to be somewhat less trusting with regard to the submissions they evaluate. In the light of recent hoaxes, perhaps we should be on the lookout for signs that authors are seeking to make journals look foolish, by having them accept outlandish claims or dodgy arguments. Perhaps, that is, we should afford the papers we read less intellectual charity, being more ready than we currently are to take counterintuitive conclusions or holes in arguments as evidence that papers should not be taken as sincere attempts to contribute to the advancement of knowledge.

3.1 Hoaxing the Journals

Hoax papers came to widespread attention with the famous Sokal hoax. In 1996, Alan Sokal, a New York University physicist, submitted a hoax paper to the journal *Social Text* (Sokal, 1996b). The article cited a range of feminist and postmodern thinkers as well as physicists, and argued that in the light of contemporary physics the idea of an external reality independent of human beings can no longer be supported. Sokal went on to argue that physics provides tools for an emancipatory political project. *Social Text* accepted the paper (allegedly, they asked for changes that Sokal refused to make; in any event, they didn't require the changes). After publication, Sokal revealed that the article was a hoax and the paper was "liberally salted with nonsense" (Sokal, 1996a).

Sokal provided a template that several others have since copied. The most notable hoax since Sokal – and the one that hits closest to home, since it targeted philosophy, as well as cultural studies – was the "grievance studies" hoax (Pluckrose, Lindsay, and Boghossian, 2018). "Grievance studies" is the name the hoaxers give to fields, like feminism and fat studies, that are as much motivated by perceived injustices as engaged in description. Like Sokal, the hoaxers wrote papers that played to editors' and reviewers' political leanings, but had a content that was allegedly nonsensical or incredible. One paper, for example, was a feminist rewrite of a chapter of *Mein Kampf*; another argued that men could reduce their transphobia by anally penetrating themselves. Despite the allegedly ludicrous or offensive contents of their papers, they succeeded in having seven accepted before exposure by the press brought the experiment to a halt.

There's no doubt that the grievance studies hoax succeeded, at least by one measure. It succeeded in reinforcing the view that the fields targeted have low intellectual standards and that in them, ideology trumps sense. It also succeeded in catapulting the authors, especially James Lindsay, to lucrative notoriety. Similarly, the Sokal hoax helped shape the opinion of the educated public, and gained Alan Sokal a degree of fame, and book contracts, he couldn't have otherwise expected. But did these hoaxes succeed in their professed aims of demonstrating that the fields targeted actually have unacceptably low standards?

While this question is a side issue, it's worth addressing it briefly – in part because we can shed light on it using tools we've developed in the previous sections. I'm not especially impressed by either hoax. *Social Text*, to which Sokal submitted "Transgressing the Boundaries," was not peer reviewed at the time. No doubt the editors of the journal found it hard to follow the paper's details, but the major ideas were clear enough: that mathematics is pervaded by ideological assumptions, that postmodern theory helps to dispel these assumptions, that contemporary mathematics provides tools that destabilize fixed meanings. The author was apparently extremely well placed to make these claims: on the one hand, he was a professor of physics at New York University; on the other, he peppered the paper with allusions and citations to influential postmodern thinkers. It's not mysterious why the editors of *Social Text* accepted the paper. It doesn't strike me as groundbreaking – the claims made, for instance the claim that Heisenberg's uncertainty principle under-mines the idea of an observer independent reality and therefore reveals physical reality to be a social construction, were commonplaces in some circles – but here they were being made by a bona fide professor of physics. As I argued in the last section, how charitably we read something, and the significance we attribute to its claims, are heavily influenced by the higher-order evidence that knowledge of the author provides us with. I think there's a strong case for thinking that the editors of *Social Text* responded appropri-ately to the evidence they had.

Social Text wasn't peer reviewed and the editors were swayed by knowledge of the author's expertise in making their decision, without the (possibly) countervailing opinions of reviewers to restrain them. But the journals Pluckrose, Lindsay, and Boghossian targeted *were* peer reviewed. Moreover, the authors didn't try to leverage the higher-order evidence provided by a prestigious appointment in a high-status field to influence editors: they submitted the papers under fictitious names, and provided "ordinary" academic affiliations. Did they succeed in casting doubt on the epistemic credentials of the fields they targeted where Sokal failed? Again, I'm skeptical.

Most of Pluckrose, Lindsay, and Boghossian's submissions (including *all* their initial submissions) were unsuccessful. They had more luck when they (a) submitted to lower-tier journals and (b) revised their papers extensively in the light of feedback, including feedback from journals that rejected them, or (c) fabricated data (Lagerspetz 2021). To my eye, the accepted papers were not obviously unworthy of acceptance at the journals they deceived. Arguably, they were genuine contributions to the fields they took aim at, either in virtue of their ideas or in virtue of the data they reported. It's noteworthy that Pluckrose, Lindsay, and Boghossian misrepresent their papers in many of their public statements (though, to be fair, they also made all papers and the records of their submissions publicly available). For example, while one paper is truly claimed to paraphrase a chapter of *Mein Kampf*, the paper follows the structure, rather than the content, of the chapter. So what?

If these reflections are right, then neither the Sokal hoax nor the grievance studies affair involved papers that were bullshit. Sokal claims his paper was "liberally salted with nonsense" and Pluckrose, Lindsay, and Boghossian (2018) aimed to produce "some little bit of lunacy or depravity," but the papers clearly have a content and might even make claims worth taking seriously. We needn't worry that reading with a sufficient degree of intellectual charity to avoid attributing bullshit will lead to false positives in cases like this. Still, these papers suggest we ought to be readier than we usually are to dismiss work as fundamentally unserious. Given the stakes, we might think, we should be on the lookout for trolls, if not for bullshit. I'm going to suggest that these hoaxes don't give us a reason to be less trusting of the papers we review. We should assume that authors intend their claims to be taken seriously, as contributions to knowledge (I'll have more to say about the attitudes authors should take to their assertions in the next section). Reviewers and editors taken in by these hoaxes shouldn't feel guilty: falling for them isn't strong grounds for concluding that they haven't fulfilled their epistemic duties.[18] Trust is essential for the functioning of peer review – and, more generally, for the growth of knowledge – and becoming less trusting threatens our capacity to acquire and transmit knowledge.

---

[18] Of course, there are possible and actual hoaxes which do reveal unacceptably low standards at the journals they target. Predatory journals pretend to enforce standards of academic rigor, but willingness to publish a paper like "Get Me Off Your Fucking Mailing List" (Safi, 2014) shreds whatever credibility they might have had.

3.2 The Epistemic Value of Trust

Setting aside our knowledge of our immediate surroundings and what we can recall about them, testimony is almost certainly the most significant route to knowledge for creatures like us. Think, for example, about how many of the facts around which people build their very identities are known to them via testimony. *He* is a *proud American*, but the fact that he lives in a nation called *the United States* is not something he could observe. *She* identifies as a Democrat, but she's aware of the existence of parties and congress only thanks to the media. *They* are fanatical about Real Madrid, though they've never been to the Bernabéu. The history of our country, the identity of the prime minister, the existence of political parties – for most of us, these are things we know only via testimony.

Testimony is vital in academic work, too. In science, most research is produced by labs, not individuals, and it's common for individual members of a research group to be unable to reproduce or sometimes even to fully understand the work produced by others. One person may have expertise in high-energy physics and make a contribution that another – say, a chemist or a medical researcher – doesn't fully understand. They must trust that the work has been done properly and that the results are reported accurately. The physicist, meanwhile, may be in precisely the same position with regard to the work of his colleagues: unable fully to understand it and taking it on trust. The researchers may not have ever met one another; not even virtually (unless making contributions to a Google document open to everyone in the group counts as "meeting"). Papers may now sometimes have literally thousands of authors, and the average number of contributors is increasing (Mallapaty, 2018).

Even within a field, trust is essential. I *might* be able to check your work, but it would be time-consuming and onerous for me to do so: *our* productivity depends on trusting one another, so that we can spend our time more efficiently and far more effectively. Trust is also required across research groups. Researchers build upon one another's findings, which they may not be able to replicate (and which they usually won't try to, for lack of time). Of course, researchers sometimes *do* set out to replicate work, especially now, in the wake of an increasing awareness that many famous studies were false positives or were p-hacked (that is, manipulated, whether nefariously or not, to produce significance). Moreover, researchers now have available statistical tools that enable them to detect fraud or error, as well as a sense of which studies are suspect (Camerer *et al.*, 2018): it's not as though results need be taken on pure faith. But even applications of these tools attest to the centrality of testimony to science. When a well-known paradigm fails a high-powered, well-conducted replication, most reputable scientists abandon it. They don't "do their own research." They don't replicate the replication. They take it largely on trust that the study was conducted as reported and that it had the results reported. Similarly, they may apply statistical tools (e.g., for estimating the degree to which effect sizes are exaggerated by publication bias) which they did not and could not develop for themselves.

Arguably, trust plays a smaller role in philosophy than in the sciences, or in history (where researchers may take on trust reports of what was found in the archives). We usually don't report results that are difficult to replicate ("Kripke Resigns As Report Alleges He Faked Results of Thought Experiments" [Fauxphilnews, 2012]) is funny because thought experiments can't be faked like that). In the next section, I discuss how philosophy makes claims that must, nevertheless, be taken on trust. For the moment, though, I want to emphasize that even setting aside the more obvious cases (x-phi data; quotation of inaccessible or translated work; descriptions of the findings of scientists in naturalistic philosophy), trust always plays some role.

Consider a thought experiment, like those that Kripke didn't fake. When a philosopher publishes a paper built around such a thought experiment, we can and do "conduct" it for ourselves. Do I have the intuition that the agent doesn't know *that's a barn*? But my response might be influenced by the context in which I encounter the thought experiment. The fact that it appears in *Journal of Really Important Philosophy* provides me with evidence that might sway me: evidence that the reviewers for JRIP, and likely its editors too, had the intuition reported. Of course, I also have evidence that the author had the intuition reported. These facts might actually help to shape my intuitions. Admittedly, the generation of intuitions is ill-understood, and some (or all) of them might be produced by cognitively impenetrable mechanisms. In that case, knowledge that *A. F. Philosopher has the intuition that the agent doesn't know* won't – directly – alter my intuitions. Still, that knowledge will affect how I respond to the case. Perhaps my intuitions aren't clear (mine often aren't). Knowing that Philosopher and the reviewers for the JRIP had the intuition might settle how seriously I take the case, despite having no clear intuition of my own. Even here, in the very heart of analytic methodology, trusting what others report makes a difference to how we respond.

Of course, we also rely on testimony (and therefore trust) with regard to the findings of subdisciplines outside our own, including findings that might constrain our interpretation of work within our own field. Just as a psychologist might prefer one theory over another because it appears to postulate mechanisms that are credibly ascribed to evolutionary history (despite having no expertise with regard to evolution), so a philosopher might reject a view because it appears to entail substance dualism (despite having little knowledge of debates over the credibility of dualism). The claim *that substance dualism is incredible* constrains their work, and this is a claim they accept on the basis of testimony.

Trust is also central to peer review. Reviewers trust the authors to report their findings, and even their intuitions, honestly. The editors trust the reviewers to read fairly and review thoughtfully. Readers trust the process has been followed, and followed competently. The need for trust pervades the entire edifice of the socially distributed enterprise that is academic research and publishing. That's part of the reason why hoaxes are so fascinating, and so challenging. That's also the reason why anything that threatens the extent to which we can trust one another threatens our capacity to produce truth and understanding. Hoaxes risk undermining the epistemic trust we have in one another (Buckwalter, 2023). Since they are damaging, and might be prevented by an increase in vigilance when we review, there's a prima facie case for reviewers becoming more suspicious.

3.3 The Fragility of Trust

Trusting someone or something consists in more than simply relying on them. We can rely on someone we don't trust. I may not set an alarm because I know I can rely on my neighbor to wake me at 6 a.m. by playing loud music. I may regard that same neighbor as too untrustworthy to nominate for the delivery of parcels when I'm out. We may rely on the untrustworthy when they have regular habits, depending on their predictability. We may also rely on tools we don't trust, when we don't have anything better to hand (Dormandy, 2020).

Standard accounts of trust hold that reliance is necessary but not sufficient for trust. Accounts of what must be added to reliance for an attitude to qualify as trust vary and I won't try to adjudicate between them. It's worth mentioning a reliable indicator by which we can distinguish mere reliance from trust: the presence of reactive attitudes (Holton, 1994). I won't feel *betrayed* if my noisy neighbor fails to wake me at 6 a.m., contrary to their usual habits. A feeling of betrayal is an indicator I trusted, rather than merely relied upon someone.

Because trust consists in reliance plus something extra, and when we trust someone we are open to being betrayed, trust exposes us to harm. Reliance already exposes us to harm: when we rely on something, we figure it into our plans (Holton, 1994), so let downs mean our interests are set back. But when we trust, we're harmed more deeply than we would have been had we merely relied upon someone: we're hurt as well as harmed. Since trust exposes us to the risk of harm, we should not trust too lightly. Since epistemic trust risks not merely our individual interests but the integrity of the academic enterprise, we'd be rational to take precautions, to weed out the untrustworthy, and to be vigilant for signs of the untrustworthy.

But while betrayals of trust set back our interests and may harm the epistemic community, vigilance, too, can damage trust. The old Russian proverb "trust, but verify" does not give us advice we can follow: attempts at verification severely damage trust on the part of the trustee, and reveals its absence on the part of the truster. As Annette Baier (1986) influentially argued, trust is "a fragile plant" and inspection of its roots tends to kill it. If I trust you, I *won't* attempt to check up on you. If Bern rings Lena's friends to verify her story that she was visiting them last night, he reveals he doesn't trust her (in that domain, at least), and Lena might feel betrayed. She will almost certainly be upset. It is not merely overt actions that damage trust; so too do epistemic precautions. Trust does not seek evidence (Jones, 1996; Hieronymi, 2008; Keren, 2020), nor does it tolerate deliberation on the evidence we have available. If betrayals of trust risk harming it, so do precautions against such betrayals.

It is, however, a familiar fact that where there is trust, there will be untrustworthy people trying to take advantage of it. And of course, the academic environment is full of people trying to take advantage of our trust: not just hoaxers, but also (and more seriously) predatory journals and conferences that will provide us with a (worthless) platform for a fee. There's a great deal wrong with the journal system as it stands. It exploits the labor of the vulnerable, it privatizes research that was often funded by public money, it's slow and often unreliable. Yet it continues to generate knowledge and understanding. That's excellent evidence that the untrustworthy have not (yet) succeeded in undermining the trust we need for the academic enterprise to keep functioning.

How have we managed to keep betrayals of trust to a sufficiently low level for the enterprise to survive, given that precautions are as, or more, damaging of trust as actual betrayal? Following Elizabeth Fricker (1994), I think at least part of the solution lies in distinguishing between implicit and explicit epistemic vigilance. While explicit vigilance – roughly, precautions we're aware of taking or deliberation we're aware of engaging in – damages trust, implicit vigilance is compatible with its preservation. There's a great deal of evidence that we are epistemically vigilant (Mascaro and Sperber, 2009; Sperber *et al.*, 2010; Harris, 2012): both children and adults weigh testimony by references to its plausibility and to its source. We give more weight to testimony that stems from those who seem benevolent toward us, to testimony that reflects a consensus view, and to testimony from those with a track record of reliability. Such weighting of testimony is automatic and subpersonal, and engaging in it is compatible with the preservation of trust.

If we're to increase our epistemic vigilance to weed out hoaxers, we might do so by taking explicit precautions. Or we might do so by increasing our implicit vigilance. I'll explore both avenues. I've already suggested that an increase in explicit vigilance risks damaging trust. I will add to that case. I'll also argue that though implicit vigilance is compatible with trust, increases in implicit vigilance risk spilling over into (damaging) explicit vigilance.

3.4 Trusting Less

Trust comes in degrees. Annuka trusts both her partner and her workmates, but she doesn't extend the same degree of trust to both. She trusts her partner to further and protect her most important interests, even when they conflict with some of his. She trusts her workmates in most contexts, but doesn't expect them to further her interests at the expense of their own. Annuka's workmates know full well that she trusts them less than she trusts her partner. They expect nothing different, and the fact that she bestows less trust on them than on him doesn't damage their relationship or decrease the trust each side has for the other.

Because trust comes in degrees without ceasing to be trust, it is in principle possible to come to trust less without becoming *dis*trusting. That being the case, we need not conclude from the fact that verification damages trust that we have no hope of becoming a little less trusting in academic contexts. We might recalibrate our explicit trust and yet preserve our epistemic commons.

Annuka's lesser trust of her workmates than her partner manifests (or consists) in two things. She trusts them in fewer spheres, and in those spheres in which she trusts them, she expects them to pay smaller costs to protect her interests. Her trust of her partner is open-ended: she expects him to take her interests into account in every context in which they're at stake. And she expects him to give her interests a significant weight across every context. Similarly, becoming less trusting in the academic sphere is likely to consist either in trusting one another in fewer spheres, or in expecting others to weigh their own interests more heavily than they currently do when they clash with our interests.

We've narrowed the spheres in which we trust one another in peer review in one way. In the wake of the replication crisis, the research community became aware of the extent of what have come to be called QRPs (questionable research practices), which fall short of fraud but which illegitimately inflate effect sizes.[19] A significant reduction in QRPs can be achieved by requiring preregistration of hypotheses and open data practices: these practices make it plain

---

[19] QRPs include generating hypotheses to explain one's data (rather than collecting data to test one's hypotheses), shelving unsuccessful trials and repeating them, adding participants to attempt to push one's results over the magical threshold of statistical significance, and splitting data in unprincipled ways. Ritchie (2020) is an insightful introduction to their misuse.

whether researchers have illegitimately manipulated their results. While there is still a great deal of resistance, some prominent journals have enthusiastically embraced the open science movement, requiring or strongly encouraging pre-registration and the availability of all data. Some journals will even commit to publishing "registered reports" on the basis of a research plan rather than a written paper (this practice results in the drafting of the skeleton of a paper that leaves conclusions open: "our analyses [confirm/failed to confirm] the hypothesis that . . ."). As a consequence, reviewers now expect authors to provide links to the preregistration and data, in the absence of which they're less willing to assume that everything was above board.

Open science practices are not designed to prevent hoaxes, but they do make them more difficult, at least when papers report data. They're not much help to most philosophers, though, or to those working in most of the rest of the humanities. There's no equivalent of manipulating data in most of our work, and no reason why we shouldn't (say) change our hypotheses midstream. There are few ways in which *we* could effectively narrow the spheres in which we trust one another. We might require that author identity be verified. That would make certain kinds of hoaxes more difficult (for example, if hoaxers use marginalized identities to give their work a credibility boost), but the effects would be small. If we're to decrease trust, we'll have to do it by reducing its degree, not its range.

Since the problem we're aiming to prevent is not fraud, but hoaxing, we might increase our vigilance for signs of its occurrence. The problem we face if we attempt to do so is that suspicion tends to snowball. In the last section, we saw how significant a difference our interpretive frame can make to how we assess a text. It's for this reason that suspicion tends to snowball: because when we're on the lookout for evidence of trolling, we won't have any difficulty in locating it.

If a hoax is to succeed, it obviously can't be too obvious. The signs we'll need to look out for must be relatively subtle. Vigilance is going to require a careful examination of the papers we review. The problem we face is that the evidence is always equivocal, and what we make of it is shaped significantly by our interpretive frame. Set yourself to discover evidence of trolling and it's all too easy to see it. The problem will be most acute in the domains in which hoaxes are most likely: arguments for counterintuitive or politically contentious conclusions.[20] Do the authors *seriously* maintain that we're living in a simulation, or that we ought to abolish the nation-state? Perhaps espousal of

---

[20] Becoming suspicious on the grounds of politically contentious conclusions (or assumptions) risks increasing epistemic injustice (Fricker, 2007), at least on certain plausible assumptions about who is most likely to hold such views. Correcting testimonial injustice seems to call for *more* trust, not less.

these views is a sign of trolling; perhaps we should increase our vigilance further? We may easily trigger a vicious cycle of suspicion, identification of potential problems, and increasing suspicion. The evidence we rely on is always equivocal – "typically the evidence we find under-determines judgments of trustworthiness or lack of trustworthiness" (O'Neill, 2020: 19) – and casting a suspicious eye over it almost guarantees we'll find signs of untrustworthiness.

When we become alert to the possibility of trolling, cued by a counterintuitive conclusion or simply because we're disposed to suspect it everywhere, every stylistic choice, every footnote, every argument might seem to indicate trouble. Is the complexity of phrasing a parody of academic verbosity? Or, on the contrary, is the simplicity deceptive? Why is the author citing *them*? What might that indicate? Suspicion is corrosive, because almost all behavior, and all writing, provides evidence that can seem to justify it given the right interpretive frame, and given a distrustful frame every piece of evidence decreases trust further. We're not, in fact, at all reliable at detecting deception in interpersonal contexts (see Shieber 2020 for a review): I suspect the same applies to the detection of hoaxes.

While trust certainly comes in degrees, explicit attempts to recalibrate it without abandoning it risk spiraling out of control. The damage such recalibration risks is almost certainly much greater, and more probable, than the risk from hoaxes. So long as hoaxes remain at a tolerably low level, it's better to remain trusting.

But alterations in *implicit* trust need not be subject to such snowballing. Implicit epistemic vigilance integrates a range of cues for reliability into a single score, by reference to which the credibility of testimony is weighted. It doesn't appear to be iterative in the way that explicit vigilance often is: that is, recalibration doesn't trigger a vicious cycle of seeming to detect evidence that supports it, thereby causing a further recalibration. We may more safely recalibrate our implicit than our explicit vigilance. Of course, we can't just *decide* to do so. But it is possible to recalibrate (some) implicit mechanisms. They're trainable: expose them to a diet of fraud and dishonesty and they're likely to become more sensitive.

Recalibrating implicit mechanisms so that they're more sensitive to evidence of hoaxing would avoid damaging trust in the way that a recalibration of explicit mechanisms risks doing: that is, the mere fact that an agent's mechanisms had thus been recalibrated wouldn't be corrosive of trust all by itself. But the effects of such a recalibration would nevertheless be negative. There are two possible outcomes of such mechanisms being triggered: either they continue to work implicitly, changing the weight we give to the claims we're assessing, or they work to trigger explicit vigilance.

If implicit mechanisms respond to cues that they parse as suspicious by alerting explicit mechanisms, they simply provide an alternative route to the same problems as a more direct recalibration of our explicit vigilance. We'd risk setting off on the corrosive cycle of suspicion, apparent confirmation, and increased suspicion.[21] But if implicit mechanisms simply work by reducing the weight we place on claims made, we risk raising the threshold for finding papers compelling enough to warrant publishing, with little gain in the detection of hoaxes. More sensitive implicit vigilance mechanisms would likely result in finding more arguments weak, more assumptions less reasonable, and so on. We'd reject hoax papers more often than we otherwise might, but only because we'd reject more often than we currently do (assuming, that is, that countervailing pressure from the journals and their need for content doesn't push us back to where we began). The problem is worse if the cues we respond to are the ones most likely to trigger explicit vigilance: counterintuitiveness and being politically contentious. We'd risk exacerbating epistemic injustice, assuming that these are claims that already struggle to get a fair hearing.

If hoaxes become frequent enough – or if journal submissions come to be saturated with deliberate bullshit through some other kind of route – we'd expect implicit *and* explicit mechanisms of epistemic vigilance to recalibrate in response. The results are likely to be very damaging for the conduct of research. Trust is fragile, and so are the institutions that depend on it. Assuming that these institutions are worth preserving, it might indeed be rational to take steps to protect them. Such steps are likely to be more effective, and so cause less damage, when they're institutional rather than individual.[22] We should not respond by becoming more vigilant; more willing to suspect bullshit in the work we review or handle as editors. Such suspicion is as or more likely to be trust-destroying as the problems it's supposed to protect us against.

4 Publication Requires Commitment

Our assessment of a text is strongly shaped by how much trust we invest in it and in the author: trust modulates intellectual charity, and higher degrees of intellectual charity entail taking the claims a text makes more seriously. In the last section, I suggested that trusting the author consists, *inter alia*, in assuming that they intend their claims to be taken seriously, as contributions to knowledge. In this section, I'll

---

[21] A related second problem is that the very training that might lead to more sensitive implicit mechanisms is likely also to make our explicit mechanisms more sensitive – and thus lead, more directly, to the same snowballing.

[22] Elsewhere, I've had a stab at describing possible institutional tweaks designed to increase (warranted) trust; for example, I've suggested that institutions should take a harsher line against those who publish in predatory journals (Levy, 2021).

defend the claim that philosophers (and other academic researchers) actually do and *should* take such an attitude to the claims they make in print. We need not *believe* the claims we defend, but we do need to commit to them as serious contributions to philosophical debate. Although we have some leeway over what doxastic attitude we may adopt (or implicate we've adopted, at any rate), we are (in most circumstances) obligated to have a positive belief attitude toward the central contentions of our papers. We must possess a belief that belongs to the range that entails (or constitutes) thinking *that it's reasonable to take this paper seriously as a contribution to philosophical debate*. This, I'll suggest, is a more demanding standard than most of those that have recently been defended as the norm governing permissible philosophical publication.

The focus here is specifically on publication and offering a paper for publication. The debate over whether philosophers need believe the claims they defend in publication builds on, but is distinct from, the debate over whether they are obligated (or even permitted) to believe their philosophical claims in general. That debate focuses in particular on what Fleisher (2020) calls "advocacy role claims" (ARCs). These are the claims philosophers make qua philosophers, rather than claims *about* philosophy. They express the views that papers aim to defend: that God is a necessary being, that free will exists, and so on. Claims about philosophy, on the other hand, are those relatively uncontroversial claims that a flat-footed history might repeat: that this is Lewis' argument for modal realism, that Dharmottara wrote a certain passage, and so on (Fleisher calls these "evidential role claims": ERCs). It's more or less uncontroversial that we are permitted to believe the ERCs we make, but there's a lively dispute right now about whether philosophers do (or should) believe their own ARCs.

The thought that philosophers need not (perhaps *should* not) believe their own ARCs is often spurred by worries about peer disagreement. It's widely accepted that agents who judge that *p* come under pressure to reduce their confidence in that judgment upon learning that *epistemic peers* – roughly, people who are as well placed to judge whether *p* – disagree with the judgment. Since our distinctively philosophical claims are *typically* contested by our epistemic peers, we therefore seem not to be entitled to believe them (DeRose, 2018; Barnett, 2019). This concern has motivated the development of accounts of sincere doxastic attitudes toward such claims that fall short of belief.

Barnett, for instance, proposes "disagreement-insulated inclination" as the appropriate attitude, where our disagreement-insulated inclinations are the way things appear to us taking into account all our evidence except the higher-order evidence stemming from the bare fact of disagreement (and perhaps some other sorts of higher-order evidence). Goldberg (2013) defends what he calls "attitudinal speculation," where one attitudinally speculates that p when one sees p as more likely than not-p, though one sees one's evidence stopping short of warranting that p. Fleisher (2021) proposes "endorsement;" a domain-specific attitude of resilient commitment and advocacy.

I'm not going to address this broader debate directly. I'm going to argue that there is no single norm of assertion governing publication in philosophy. Rather, there's a range. In offering a paper for publication, we act as guarantor that it's worth readers' time; we thereby implicate that we regard it as, at minimum, reasonably taken seriously as a contribution to philosophy. This guarantee is given by implicating some degree of commitment to the claims made; the stronger the commitment implicated the more strongly we imply that it is worth our readers' time, effort, and intellectual charity. We implicate that we have a pro-attitude toward it that entails that we *believe* it is a serious contribution to philosophical debate. In doing so, we offer *evidence* for our ARCs: since that's the case, we're obliged to actually possess the attitude we implicate (or, at any rate, a sufficiently similar attitude). To fail to possess such an attitude would be to present misleading evidence, and that is impermissible in most ordinary circumstances.

4.1 With or without Belief?

While there is a fairly extensive literature on whether philosophers should or do believe the distinctively philosophical propositions they assert, until recently none of that literature focused specifically on publication. As Alexandra Plakias (2019) notes, however, the norms that govern publication might be different from the norms that govern discussion in the classroom or the seminar room. For one thing, in the face-to-face context there may be more opportunity to work through qualifications and caveats; for another, the stakes are very different (given the role that publication plays in getting and keeping jobs in philosophy). Whatever the appropriate norms in philosophical discussion, Plakias argues, we may permissibly *publish* without belief.

Plakias (2019: 638–639) describes three (realistic) cases in which philosophers might publish without belief.

Malicious Deceiver: In order to expose its lax editorial standards, Ben submits a paper to a journal arguing for a view he considers patently absurd.

Repentant (non)Realist: Sanjay publishes a paper called "A defence of non-naturalism," outlining a compelling response to the central objections against the view. Sanjay believes nonnaturalism is implausible but doesn't mention this fact in the paper.

Doubtful Graduate: Rachel publishes an argument against a popular position, based on empirical research she fears might turn out to be unreliable. Furthermore, she's not confident that the position she's criticizing is false.

Plakias expects us to share her intuition that all three cases are permissible.[23] She also provides several arguments why that intuition is the right one. She argues that making belief a requirement on publication would skew the field against conciliationists (that is, those who hold that we ought to reduce our confidence that *p* in the face of peer disagreement): since conciliationism often (or always) entails that we should not believe our controversial philosophical views, accepting the norm that we ought to publish only when we're believers ensures that conciliationists would get few opportunities to publish. More generally, it would ensure that philosophers with lower standards for belief tend to be overrepresented in the literature, which would be bad on epistemic consequentialist grounds. In very recent work, she adds that it would also skew the field against agents who lack confidence in themselves, which (as she suggests) is unjust, given that a lack of self-confidence reflects a history of marginalization (Plakias, 2023).

Plakias argues that there is in fact no norm of philosophical publication; there's no attitude that philosophers are obliged to adopt toward the claims they make in their papers. What matters is the *argument*, not the author's attitude toward it. "The writer's own belief is beside the point" (Plakias, 2019: 644). The argument must stand or fall on its own. What matters is that the claim *is* reasonable to believe, and that is secured by the provision of a sufficiently good argument, not by the author's attitude to it. A philosopher permissibly publishes a distinctively philosophical claim if that claim is reasonable to believe, whether or not *they* believe it or is even entitled to believe it.

Fleisher (2020) endorses Plakias' contention that the argument ought largely to stand on its own (he suggests that norms governing ARCs are extrinsic: norms that are shaped by the promotion of healthy inquiry). He notes, however, that we need not provide an argument for our ERCs. Philosophers publish this kind of claim "with the aim of having their audience believe it on trust" (Fleisher, 2020: 241). As we noted in the last section, testimony, more or less on its own, warrants acceptance of some of the claims made in philosophical articles. Fleisher (2020: 243) suggests that ERCs are "claims that aim or function to increase the common stock of evidence available to enquirers";

---

[23] Malicious Deceiver is explicitly modelled on the "grievance studies" hoax discussed in the previous section. I'm doubtful the case was permissible. But such hoaxes can be permissible, when they genuinely expose indefensible academic standards. Let's stipulate that Ben has a well-justified belief that editorial standards at the journal he submits to are absurdly lax and that he has good reason to think no one who is not knowingly complicit in bad behavior will be harmed by his actions.

with regard to them, the norm of publication is justifiable belief. For example, it's impermissible for an author to assert in print that they have gathered empirical data unless they justifiably believe they have.

Fleisher is right in thinking that different norms govern ERCs and ARCs. Before turning to my own views, however, let me note that Fleisher's justified belief norm for ERCs is too demanding. Consider a version of Malicious Deceiver in which the hoaxer claims to have gathered empirical data that is patently absurd (suppose they report that 92 percent of registered Democrats switched their political allegiance to Donald Trump when primed with a picture of a kitten). Were a journal to publish a paper built around these results, the hoaxer would have succeeded in exposing its lax editorial standards. Closer to (philosophical) home, someone might presuppose what they call "the theory of motivation developed by David Hume" in mounting an argument, while believing that the common attribution of such a theory to Hume is mistaken. Such an assertion is permissible, if it is true that (a) such a theory is commonly attributed to Hume (such that by identifying it with his views, one picks out a well understood view), and (b) it is the theory itself, and not the attribution to Hume, that does philosophical work.

Further, making justified belief the norm of publication for ERCs would skew the field against those with high standards for belief (just as making belief the norm of publication for distinctively philosophical claims would skew the field against conciliationists). Consider Keita, a researcher who conducts an experimental study using participants sourced through Amazon Turk. Keita has scrupulously examined the literature on the reliability and replicability of data gathered on the platform and has carefully framed her research questions and participant exclusion criteria to eliminate problems. Nevertheless, she worries about the possibility of bots and random response, and can't quite bring herself to believe her own data is accurate. Rather, she regards it as meeting the standards accepted in her field for reliability and sees those standards as defensible. Keita publishes permissibly, despite failing to believe the ERCs she makes.

4.2 A Plea for Charity

Fleisher agrees that the norms of publication that govern the cases Plakias presents are very undemanding. Since they centrally involve the assertion of ARCs, they stand or fall on their own merits, and philosophers' attitudes matter only to the extent ERCs are at issue. However, features of the very cases Plakias uses to motivate her argument suggest that the attitude philosophers take to their ARCs matters more than either she or Fleisher thinks. Plakias (2019: 641) herself notes that in a realistic version of *Repentant (non)Realist*, Sanjay would probably keep his genuine attitude to himself, since "he might reasonably expect that such a caveat would negatively affect his chances of publication." Similarly, she notes, Rachel the doubtful graduate does well to keep quiet about her worries about the research she relies on. But if there is no requirement that we believe our philosophical views, why should confession negatively affect our papers' chances? If nothing matters but the argument, such confessions should be neither here nor there.

Hoaxes like *Malicious Deceiver* owe much of their success in delegitimizing journals to the attitudes of their authors. It's *because the paper was intended as a joke* that the journal is supposed to look ridiculous, not merely *because the paper was bad*. Author attitude *does* make a difference here. The point generalizes: arguments *don't* stand on their own, independent of their authors' attitudes.

Philosophy papers aim to establish claims through sufficiently compelling arguments; since we provide such arguments for our ARCs, our attitudes toward them matter very much less than our attitudes toward claims we warrant by testimony alone. But as we saw in previous sections, all kinds of factors, about context and content, make a justifiable difference to argument strength. Implicated author attitude is one of these factors: how compelling we find the argument is and should to some degree be affected by how seriously it is advanced as a candidate for truth.

When we advance an ARC, we don't vouch for its truth or even its plausibility. Rather, we vouch, roughly, *this is worth your time*. Time and attention are limited resources, and we justifiably ask readers to expend these resources on following and assessing our arguments when we implicate that we're prepared to stand by them, in some sense. By asserting ARCs, we implicate that the argument we offer is a serious contribution to philosophical conversation; we implicate, that is, that *we* take a certain attitude to it. We do not need to believe the claims we defend, nor even implicate that we believe them. But in offering a paper for publication, we certify that we regard them as reasonably seen as following from reasonably, or actually, accepted premises, and – therefore – that our ARCs constitute a serious contribution to philosophical debate.

It's noteworthy that this standard doesn't specify the strength of the attitude we must take to our claims. We might permissibly believe them (conciliationist considerations aside), or find them compelling, or we might adopt some weaker attitude. Indeed, philosophers are sometimes open in saying that they don't believe the upshot of their own argument: for instance, Lycan (2009) devotes a paper to defending substance dualism from the objections leveled against it, while confessing he is utterly unconvinced by dualism. When philosophers do this, they explicitly ask us seriously to consider an argument for a conclusion that they're unwilling to vouch for themselves. Nevertheless, they represent themselves as taking the argument to be reasonably believed, or reasonably held to follow from premises that are reasonably, or widely, believed.[24] Sanjay and Rachel might permissibly have advanced their arguments in this spirit. Rachel might have said that if a certain set of research findings are true (about which she has doubts) then a popular position faces hitherto unrecognized problems; Sanjay might have noted that he aims to show that popular objections to it fail, not that nonnaturalism is true. They might have done these things, but they didn't because they know that their chances of publication would have been reduced had they been more open about their doubts. Why is that the case, given that their arguments would have been just as strong, and they would have satisfied the norms on philosophical publication?

Expressions of attitude strength make a difference to our paper's chances of success for familiar reasons: because they figure among the extra-argumentative features of content and context that modulate the degree of intellectual charity with which readers (including reviewers) approach papers. Confess yourself unconvinced by your own argument and readers will justifiably expend less effort in processing it (other things being equal). Even presenting a claim as reasonably accepted conditional on some other claim being true will result in a less charitable reading, especially if one confesses oneself agnostic about the other claim.

Because we may reasonably ask our readers to extend varying degrees of charity to our arguments, there is no single norm for philosophical publication. Rather, there's a range, and representing oneself as holding that distinctively philosophical claims are reasonably held to follow from widely or reasonably held premises represents the minimum threshold for publication in normal cases. In certifying that we take this attitude to our claims (which we do by offering it for publication), we vouch that it is worth the reader's time. But time (and effort and attention – which are some of the constituents of intellectual charity) are open-ended. Publication implicates *this is worth your time*; other things being equal, publications that assert *I take this to be true* implicate that the argument is worth more sustained thought.

It's not a mere brute fact that that the expression of attitudes makes a difference to intellectual charity: it's a rational response. Other things being equal, we should think that an argument its own author takes to be

---

[24] In the latter kind of case – when a philosopher advances an argument that depends on actually accepted premises – she may not herself share the belief in these premises and may in fact regard them as unreasonable. Such an argument might be explicitly presented as a *reductio* of a common view, but it need not. Sometimes the philosopher is agnostic about the premises but keeps quiet about that to boost the chances that those who are committed to them will take the argument seriously. Still, she truthfully implicates that she takes the paper to be worth readers' time.

unpersuasive is worth less effort than a more successful argument: given the (defeasible) link between being persuasive and actually persuading the attentive reader, the author's being persuaded by an argument signals their perception of its persuasive power and thereby that it is worth investing time in it. For the same reason, asserting that an argument is successful also calls on the reader to approach it with more intellectual charity. Interesting philosophical arguments (outside logic) do not follow indubitably from undeniable premises. Most do not deductively establish their conclusions; rather they make them more or less plausible. We should expect our readers to take them more seriously, put more effort into them, and regard them as more credible candidates for truth when we assert or imply that we believe them (imagine a paper in which the intuition that p plays a pivotal role, but the author reports not sharing that intuition).

When we can do so in good conscience, we therefore assert or imply that we believe our philosophical claims. If we have high standards for belief, accept a demanding conciliationism, or if we simply aren't sure whether our credence in a view qualifies as belief, we may assert or imply something weaker (but still stronger than merely "this is worth your time" if we don't stray too far from our genuine attitude). Between outright belief and the weakest condition on permissible publication (being believed to be reasonable to believe or reasonably held to follow from reasonably or widely held premises), there is an indefinitely large range, and our implicated attitude may permissibly fall anywhere in that range (except when special features of the ARCs dictate that some stretches of the range are off-limits: because they would generate Moore paradoxicality, perhaps, or would be self-undermining). There is no one norm governing publication of distinctively philosophical claims; rather, there is a range with a lower bound. The stronger the commitment to our ARCs we implicate, the greater the degree of intellectual charity we ask our readers to extend toward them; since in doing so, we offer evidence for our claims, readers will tend to modulate their charity accordingly.

It's worth noting that this proposal avoids the worry about belief that arises from conciliationist intuitions. It might be true that we are not rationally permitted to believe our ARCs in the face of peer disagreement, but since peer disagreements over whether arguments are worth taking seriously as contributions to philosophical debate are much rarer than peer disagreement over their conclusions, we are usually rationally permitted to believe that our argument is worth readers' time, regardless of the truth of conciliationism. However, the proposal still faces a serious worry: the worry Plakias (2023) emphasizes in her very recent contribution to the debate. Confidence is neither equally nor fairly distributed, and any norm on permissible publication risks heightening the unfairness. It places those who are less confident at a disadvantage, and that often compounds unfairness.[25]

The attitude we implicate toward our own ARCs makes a justifiable difference to the degree of intellectual charity with which they're read because in implicating that attitude we provide genuine (higher-order) *evidence* for them. In this light, the question "may we permissibly put forward claims as serious contributions to philosophical discussion when we don't in fact believe they count as such contributions?" is equivalent to "may we permissibly misrepresent our evidence?" Putting it in these terms heightens the problem just mentioned, suggesting we face a trade-off between purely epistemic values and fairness.

While I think that we do face such a trade-off (I'll have more say about such trade-offs in the concluding section), I don't think we face a stark choice between narrowly epistemic goods and fairness. We are not epistemically obligated to represent our commitments with absolute fidelity; rather, we are obligated to avoid too flagrant a misrepresentation of our attitude. We're obligated to avoid implicating that readers should invest much more time and attention in our arguments than we think they deserve. We have leeway to put the best face we can on our claims. As we've seen, such leeway is commonly exploited, and its exploitation is accepted. Sanjay implicates a stronger commitment to nonnaturalism than he actually possesses and Rachel allows the reader to think she has a reasonably high credence in the empirical evidence she cites; neither faces censure if they subsequently admit the spin they've engaged in. But too flagrant a misrepresentation of authorial attitude and the reader would feel betrayed upon learning of it, because they've been asked to invest time and effort into assessing an argument under false pretenses.[26] Authors like Rachel and Sanjay are almost always careful to hedge, implicating a higher

---

[25] Buckwalter (2023) is the only prominent defense of a belief norm for publishing. Buckwalter points out that accepting less stringent norms for publication to level the playing field for those who are conciliationists wouldn't solve a more general problem, since it would still leave those with less stringent standards for (say) evidence at an advantage. The solution, he argues, is to have a single, demanding norm apply to everyone. That solution ignores the problem of lack of confidence highlighted by Plakias. A demanding belief norm would inadvertently reinforce the marginalization that in many cases underlies a lack of confidence. My proposal, which allows people to implicate a degree of commitment somewhat greater than they feel, seems to have most of the advantages of Buckwalter's belief norm without the drawbacks. Nor is it as revisionary as Buckwalter's proposal (he seems to assume that the belief norm currently prevails; I'm confident that something closer to my proposal is actually nearer the prevailing norm).

[26] It's no accident that it tends to be senior people like Lycan who openly signal their lack of commitment to their ARCs, whereas graduate students like Rachel must be more circumspect. Someone like Lycan can rely on their well-established reputation to warrant the value of their arguments without needing the additional boost that comes from commitment.

degree of commitment than they actually feel but avoiding asserting outright belief.

We are rationally permitted to put a positive spin on our attitudes toward our claims, so long as we do not so flagrantly misrepresent them as to ask readers to invest a degree of time, effort, and attention that is heavily disproportionate to the degree the author believes is warranted. Just as Sanjay may permissibly imply a degree of commitment to nonnaturalism he doesn't genuinely feel, and Rachel may downplay her skepticism about the experimental data she cites, so the underconfident author may permissibly imply a higher credence in the success, and the worth, of their argument than they genuinely possess. They do not betray readers' trust so long as the disproportion between the amount of intellectual charity they call for and their genuine attitudes is not excessive. Were Rachel to be really confident that the data was junk, she'd be obliged to present her argument more cautiously. Equally, the underconfident author violates readers' and reviewers' trust by submitting a paper they genuinely believe to be worthless. Impostor syndrome is a real and widespread phenomenon, and it's not at all unusual for people to *suspect* or *fear* that their work is not worth reading. Fortunately, these attitudes allow leeway for positive spin, consistent with submission to journals.[27]

I've suggested that the norm of publication, and even submission for publication, is commitment. But aren't hoaxers like Malicious Deceiver counterexamples? While I've suggested that the Sokal hoax and the grievance studies hoax were of dubious permissibility, I've also allowed that hoaxes can be permissible. Consider the sting operation aimed at predatory journals, revealing their willingness to publish garbage for a fee (Bohannon, 2013). Hoaxers don't assert claims they regard as reasonably believed. They may sometimes assert claims they take as reasonably held to follow from widely accepted premises (perhaps they aim to show how ridiculous these premises are) but that would capture only a minority of permissible hoaxes. Hoaxers might instead think that the fields they aim to expose draw bizarre conclusions from reasonable

---

[27] The norm of publication still leaves the underconfident at a disadvantage. It's worth noting that this disadvantage arises somewhat independently of the norm: ordinary people assign greater credibility to confident testifiers than to the less confident (Price and Stone, 2004; Pulford *et al.*, 2018). The confidence heuristic is rational, since (other things being equal) it makes sense to match one's credences to the credences of those who testify. But confidence can be unearned and lack of confidence may reflect oppressive socialization or a history of testimonial injustice. Confidence is good evidence only with background conditions held constant: unconfident testimony from a member of a marginalized group may be as good or better evidence than confident testimony from members of a historically privileged group. Of course, anonymous review strips out this background information, leaving us unable to take it into account in calibrating credence.

premises. Nor need hoaxers believe that the claims they assert are worth readers' time and effort.

I think these cases inform us about the *scope* of the norms for permissible publication, rather than their *content*. Whatever the norms of assertion are for claims made in ordinary interactions, we need not abide by them when we don't owe our interlocutor sincerity, let alone truth, and important goals can be achieved by insincere or unjustifiable assertion. The murderer at the door is not owed truth. Similarly, predatory journals, and those that publish pseudoscience, aren't owed the truth and we might better advance our epistemic goals by lying to them. Malicious Deceiver provides insight into *when* the norms of assertion are and are not in place, not what these norms are.[28]

In closing this section, let me note how this account diverges in its basis from those put forward by Plakias, Fleisher, and also Barnett (2019). All three justify their accounts on the basis of consequentialist considerations: they advocate norms of sincerity that will best advance philosophical inquiry. I suspect that the stronger norm of assertion I've urged here is also justifiable on this kind of basis. Calibrating our investment of time and effort by reference to such cues (while remaining somewhat sensitive to evidence that they're insincere) leads to a better community-wide division of labor. However, that's not the basis from which these norms draw their normative force. Author attitude is *evidence*, and the relevant norms are epistemic: we're misrepresenting our evidence when we pretend to a degree of confidence that is far greater than our actual attitude. Unless we're in a situation in which there is no justified expectation of honesty, we are required to present our evidence honestly. Philosophy can be proud: to the litany of QRPs we're familiar with from the experimental sciences (HARKing – hypothesizing after the results are known, p-hacking, data dredging, and the rest) we can add one of our own: misrepresenting the evidence by failing to report that we ourselves don't take our ARCs to be worth readers' time.

5 In Lieu of a Conclusion

I began with a promise to discuss the question that increasingly preoccupies professional philosophers: Why was my paper rejected? While this Element has ranged over some surprising territory, far from the considerations that feature in

---

[28] Fleisher (2020) notes that Malicious Deceiver is more controversial than Plakias' other cases. I think the remarks in this paragraph help clarify just why the case is controversial. The controversy arises from differing views on (a) whether the journals targeted (and reviewers for them) are owed the kind of respect we manifest in asserting claims sincerely and (b) if they are not, whether the means chosen caused minimal harm, compared to the good generated.

the deliberations of reviewers and editors, it is unified by threads that help us to answer that question.

The central theme is the difference that intellectual charity makes to our evaluation of texts. The difference can be very dramatic, causing us to see a tolerably clear claim as literally meaningless. More often, and more relevantly, the differences are much smaller – but in peer review, small differences are often decisive. Revise and resubmits turn on fine margins, and most papers that get them might easily have been rejected. A slightly less charitable reading, and almost every revise and resubmit could have been a reject.

Few people will be surprised by the suggestion that intellectual charity plays this often decisive role. Much more controversially, I've suggested that we respond rationally to features of text and context in modulating the degree of charity with which we read, and that some of the features we respond to modulate the *quality* of the text, even though they may not be intrinsic to it. Quality, I've suggested, is a partly relational property, and arguments don't stand on their own in the way philosophers like to imagine. The attitude that *others* take to an argument, the attitude the author purports to take to it, its reception history, the context in which it appears – all these factors appropriately alter how seriously we take it, both by giving us a sense of the qualities the text possessed all along, and by helping to constitute its value. These factors can transform an otherwise unsuccessful argument into one that is persuasive.

Let me demonstrate the utility of this framework by applying it to a brief discussion of two complaints that are often heard about peer review: that it favors conservative, technically competent papers over innovative ones, and that anonymous review is a façade, with senior people getting an easier ride from reviewers. I don't know whether either is true, but if they are, both are rationally explicable by the kinds of factors I've invoked.

There's some evidence for a conservative bias in peer review (Arvan, Bright, and Heesen, 2022), though the evidence doesn't directly concern philosophy. In any case, a conservative bias is exactly what we would expect. As we saw, a counterintuitive thesis typically causes readers to reduce their intellectual charity. Indeed, it's common for philosophers to explicitly invoke some sort of conservatism as a theoretical virtue: it's common to regard a conflict with common sense as a pro tanto reason to reject a view. Quine thought this kind of conservatism was justified only by our psychological preferences, but in fact it may be rationally justifiable within a Bayesian framework: views that conflict with the assessor's prior beliefs face a higher justificatory bar. Of course, belief update is appropriately sensitive to our priors. So the decrease in charity is a justifiable response to a counterintuitive thesis.[29]

It may be that the magnitude of reviewer conservatism is greater than a narrow Bayesianism can explain. We might expect reviewers who are unpersuaded by papers on Bayesian grounds to nevertheless recommend them for publication more often than they actually do, because they aim at other epistemic and nonepistemic goods: novelty, diversity of perspectives, and so on. But if intra- and extratextual properties make them not merely more skeptical but also less charitable, then they will tend to reject innovative papers even more often, no matter their motivations. They will tend to see these papers as not merely false, but also as less interesting or careful or otherwise valuable than they might have.

We can also explain the (alleged) easy ride that big names get by reference to intellectual charity. Even when journals practice anonymous review (as almost all philosophy journals do), reviewers sometimes know or guess who the author is, especially when they're a big name. Big names are more likely to develop well-established frameworks, and may have recognizable styles: even when they're careful to conceal their identity, competent reviewers may recognize the framework being developed, or even have heard the paper at a conference.[30] As we've seen, author identity can be a factor that justifiably modulates the degree of charity with which a reviewer reads: *of course* I should think what Big Name writes is worth reading with care, and *of course* I should work to resolve any apparent confusions or inconsistencies I take myself to detect.

Intellectual charity enters into a further stage of the reviewing process, one we haven't discussed. A reviewer's report is itself a text that can be read more or less charitably, with charity extended to both the reviewer and to the text on which it reports. Editors are much more likely than reviewers to know author identity, since few philosophy journals practice triple anonymous review. Editors therefore read both the paper and the reports from within an interpretive framework that is sensitive to the identity of their authors. When they respect the author more than the reviewer (for example), they're more likely to attribute confusion to the review than the paper.

Is this unfair? It certainly is. It's multiply unfair: *even if* Big Name's paper is better than yours, that very fact probably reflects the many advantages Big

---

[29] Think of the so-called Sagan standard: extraordinary claims require extraordinary evidence. The standard follows directly from Bayesianism combined with the (overwhelmingly plausible) idea that extraordinary claims have low prior probability. Steven Bland (in press) suggests that a failure to be as sufficiently conservative as Bayesianism recommends is partly to blame for the current replication crisis.

[30] Reviewers seem to overestimate their success at guessing author identity, but they certainly sometimes succeed in doing so (Fisher, Friedman, and Strauss, 1994; Snodgrass, 2006).

Name, with their light teaching load and ample research assistance, has over you. That's a kind of unfairness that is inherent even in a fully meritocratic publishing system, and one that we may have to live with. But it's also unfair for other reasons. For one thing, Big Name might not deserve their reputation; so long as academic goods remain responsive to prestige *independent from* quality, credibility boosts might be unfair (though nevertheless assigned rationally). Even when Big Name genuinely is my epistemic superior, and therefore it is rationally justifiable to read their work with more intellectual charity than mine, most of us believe that some sort of equality of opportunity should prevail in publishing. Perhaps we ought to sacrifice the slight veritistic edge that arises from giving epistemic superiors an easier ride in favor of other goods, like equality of opportunity and a diversity of voices. Triple anonymous review might be justifiable *not* because it's irrational to give big names an easier ride, but to promote these other goods.[31]

It's worth noting, however, that we might face a dilemma. The more we level the playing field, the more conservative we might make peer review. Here's why: if it is true that reviewers and editors are significantly more likely to assess really innovative papers with sufficient charity to recommend revise and resubmits when the author is known to be an established philosopher than when they're a relative unknown, hiding author identity might ensure that really innovative papers are published even less frequently in the future than they are currently. Whether we face such a trade-off, and to what extent we'd diminish one good in favor of another, are partly empirical questions. We should pursue a diversity of models, and measure the strengths and weaknesses of each.

If the framework I've developed here has value, it might be in allowing us to glimpse what trade-offs we face, and therefore what qualities we should measure in assessing different models. There are legitimate concerns about peer review that are not epistemic. We might ask, for example, what role it plays in shaping the character of the philosophical profession and in who gets to count as an expert. Pursuing narrowly epistemic goods through peer review may come at a cost of a less welcoming and less just profession. These sorts of trade-offs are pervasive, and to some degree inevitable. Walter Benjamin famously wrote "[t]here is no document of civilization which is not at the same time a document of barbarism" (Benjamin, 2019: 256); something like this dictum holds in peer review (just for a start, philosophical excellence reflects and reinforces unearned privilege).

---

[31] One problem with the repository model recommended by Heesen and Bright (2020), and more implicitly by Arvan, Bright, and Heesen (2022), is that it risks increasing the power of author identity to sway interpretation. I worry that papers by established authors would have significantly more readers *and* be read significantly more charitably than papers by graduate students and new PhDs.

There's no algorithm for negotiating these trade-offs. Sometimes we ought to emphasize epistemic goods over other values, sometimes the reverse, and there's plenty of room for reasonable disagreement over cases. While I am very confident that some trade-offs are inevitable, I am equally confident that it is sometimes possible to avoid them and always possible to minimize them. We should certainly explore ways of redesigning or replacing peer review with these goals in mind.

It's also worth noting that I've focused on short-term epistemic evaluation, largely at the level of the individual paper. That focus brackets important and genuinely epistemic questions about debates, fields, and even society at large. Sometimes, trading off epistemic values *now* favors epistemic value *later*; for example, by promoting a diversity of perspectives. Proposals for the redesign or replacement of peer review needs to be assessed against these criteria, too.

I'm hopeful the proliferation of norms, criteria, works, venues, and approaches I've called for might go some way toward minimizing the trade-offs. More diverse criteria and a more diverse profession might by themselves lead to a profession that is less likely to lurch from hot topic to hot topic, and a better allocation of epistemic resources, while helping to reduce some of the nonepistemic injustices that remain so prevalent. Can we have documents of civilization that are not also documents of barbarism? Perhaps not, but nor need we accept every barbarism as the price of civilization.

References

Arvan, M., Bright, L. K., and Heesen, R. (2022) "Jury Theorems for Peer Review," *British Journal for the Philosophy of Science* [preprint]. https://doi.org/10.1086/719117.

Baier, A. (1986) "Trust and Antitrust | Ethics," *Ethics*, 96(2), pp. 231–260.

Balibar, E. (2014) *The Philosophy of Marx*. Verso Books.

Barnett, Z. (2019) "Philosophy without Belief," *Mind*, 128(509), pp. 109–138. https://doi.org/10.1093/mind/fzw076.

Benjamin, W. (2019) *Illuminations: Essays and Reflections*. Houghton Mifflin Harcourt.

Bennett, J. (1982) "A Note on Interpretation," *Canadian Journal of Philosophy*, 12(4), pp. 753–755. https://doi.org/10.1080/00455091.1982.10715814.

Bland, S. (in press) *Rationality in Context: Unstable Virtues in an Uncertain World*. Routledge.

Bohannon, J. (2013) "Who's Afraid of Peer Review?," *Science*, 342(6154), pp. 60–65. https://doi.org/10.1126/science.342.6154.60.

Bourdieu, P. (1998) *The State Nobility: Elite Schools in the Field of Power*. Stanford University Press.

Buckwalter, W. (2023) "The Belief Norm of Academic Publishing," *Ergo: An Open Access Journal of Philosophy*, 9(54). https://doi.org/10.3998/ergo.3117.

Camerer, C. F., Dreber, A., Holzmeister, F., *et al.* (2018) "Evaluating the Replicability of Social Science Experiments in *Nature* and *Science* between 2010 and 2015," *Nature Human Behaviour*, 2(9), pp. 637–644. https://doi.org/10.1038/s41562-018-0399-z.

Campbell, J. (1980) "Locke on Qualities," *Canadian Journal of Philosophy*, 10 (4), pp. 567–585. https://doi.org/10.1080/00455091.1980.10715745.

Clark, A. and Chalmers, D. J. (1998) "The Extended Mind," *Analysis*, 58(1), pp. 7–19. https://doi.org/10.1093/analys/58.1.7.

Cohen, G. A. (2002) "Deeper into Bullshit," in S. Buss and L. Overton (eds.) *Contours of Agency*. MIT Press, pp. 331–339.

Cohen, G. A. (2013) "Complete Bullshit," in *Finding Oneself in the Other*. Princeton University Press, pp. 94–114.

"Colorless Green Ideas Sleep Furiously" (2022), *Wikipedia*. https://en.wikipedia.org/w/index.php?title=Colorless_green_ideas_sleep_furiously&oldid=1124886786 (Accessed: December 14, 2022).

De Cruz, H. (2018) "Prestige Bias: An Obstacle to a Just Academic Philosophy," *Ergo: An Open Access Journal of Philosophy*, 5. http://dx.doi.org/10.3998/ergo.12405314.0005.010.

DeRose, K. (2018) *The Appearance of Ignorance*. Oxford University Press.

Dormandy, K. (2020) "Introduction: An Overview of Trust and Some Key Epistemological Implications," in K. Dormandy (ed.) *Trust in Epistemology*. Routledge, pp. 1–40.

Dotson, K. (2013) "How Is This Paper Philosophy?," *Comparative Philosophy*, 3(1), pp. 3–29.

Driver, J. and Rosati, C. (2021) "From the Editors," *Ethics*, 132(1), pp. 1–3. https://doi.org/10.1086/715390.

Dutilh Novaes, C. (2013) "Is Peer-Reviewing Really Tracking Quality in Philosophy?," *New APPS: Art, Politics, Philosophy, Science*, September 24. www.newappsblog.com/2013/09/is-peer-reviewing-really-tracking-quality-in-philosophy.html (Accessed: December 29, 2021).

Dutilh Novaes, C. (2020) "The Role of Trust in Argumentation," *Informal Logic*, 40(2), pp. 205–236. https://doi.org/10.22329/il.v40i2.6328.

fauxphilnews (2012) "Kripke Resigns As Report Alleges He Faked Results of Thought Experiments," *fauxphilnews*, February 23. https://fauxphilnews.wordpress.com/2012/02/22/kripke-resigns-after-allegations-of-academic-fraud/ (Accessed: February 1, 2022).

Fernandez-Duque, D., Evans, J., and Hodges, C. C. (2015) "Superfluous Neuroscience Information Makes Explanations of Psychological Phenomena More Appealing," *Journal of Cognitive Neuroscience*, 27(5), pp. 926–944. https://doi.org/10.1162/jocn_a_00750.

Fisher, M., Friedman, S. B., and Strauss, B. (1994) "The Effects of Blinding on Acceptance of Research Papers by Peer Review," *JAMA*, 272(2), pp. 143–146. https://doi.org/10.1001/jama.1994.03520020069019.

Fleisher, W. (2020) "Publishing without (Some) Belief," *Thought*, 9(4), pp. 237–246.

Fleisher, W. (2021) "How to Endorse Conciliationism," *Synthese*, 198, pp. 9913–9939. https://doi.org/10.1007/s11229-020-02695-z.

Frankfurt, H. G. (2002) "Reply to G. A. Cohen," in S. Buss and L. Overton (eds.) *Contours of Agency*. MIT Press, pp. 340–344.

Frankfurt, H. G. (2009) *On Bullshit*. Princeton University Press.

Fricker, E. (1994) "Against Gullibility," in A. Chakrabarti and B. K. Matilal (eds.) *Knowing from Words*. Kluwer Academic Publishers.

Fricker, M. (2007) *Epistemic Injustice: Power and the Ethics of Knowing*. Oxford University Press.

Fritz, J. (2018) "Conciliationism and Moral Spinelessness," *Episteme*, 15(1), pp. 101–118. https://doi.org/10.1017/epi.2016.44.

Gadamer, H.-G. (1975) *Truth and Method*. Seabury Press.

Gans, J. S. and Shepherd, G. B. (1994) "How Are the Mighty Fallen: Rejected Classic Articles by Leading Economists," *Journal of Economic Perspectives*, 8(1), pp. 165–179.

Gettier, E. L. (1963) "Is Justified True Belief Knowledge?," *Analysis*, 23(6), pp. 121–123. https://doi.org/10.1093/analys/23.6.121.

Goldberg, S. (2013) "Defending Philosophy in the Face of Systematic Disagreement," in D. E. Machuca (ed.) *Disagreement and Skepticism*. Routledge, pp. 277–294.

Goldhill, O. (2016) "Why Are So Many Smart People Such Idiots about Philosophy?," *Quartz*, March 6. https://qz.com/627989/why-are-so-many-smart-people-such-idiots-about-philosophy/ (Accessed: June 27, 2021).

Goldhill, O. (2017) "We Asked Deepak Chopra, the Guru of Sayings That Mean Nothing, to Fact-Check His Own Tweets," *Quartz*, March 5. https://qz.com/917820/we-asked-deepak-chopra-the-guru-of-sayings-that-mean-nothing-to-fact-check-his-own-tweets/ (Accessed: February 14, 2022).

Haddad, S. (2016) "A Petty Pedagogy? Teaching Philosophy in Derrida's 'Cogito and the History of Madness'," in O. Custer, P. Deutscher, and S. Haddad (eds.) *Foucault/Derrida Fifty Years Later: The Futures of Genealogy, Deconstruction, and Politics*. Columbia University Press, pp. 133–148. https://doi.org/10.7312/columbia/9780231171953.003.0008.

Harman, G. (2009) *Prince of Networks: Bruno Latour and Metaphysics*. re. press.

Harris, P. (2012) *Trusting What You're Told*. Harvard University Press.

Hedden, B. (2019) "Hindsight Bias Is Not a Bias," *Analysis*, 79(1), pp. 43–52. https://doi.org/10.1093/analys/any023.

Heesen, R. and Bright, L. K. (2020) "Is Peer Review a Good Idea?," *British Journal for the Philosophy of Science*, 72(3), p. axz029. https://doi.org/10.1093/bjps/axz029.

Hieronymi, P. (2008) "The Reasons of Trust," *Australasian Journal of Philosophy*, 86(2), pp. 213–236. https://doi.org/10.1080/00048400801886496.

Holton, R. (1994) "Deciding to Trust, Coming to Believe," *Australasian Journal of Philosophy*, 72(1), pp. 63–76. https://doi.org/10.1080/00048409412345881.

Hoogeveen, S., Haaf, J. M., Bulbulia, J. A., *et al.* (2022) "The Einstein Effect: Global Evidence for Scientific Source Credibility Effects and the Influence of Religiosity," *Nature Human Behaviour*, 6(4), pp. 523–535. https://doi.org/10.1038/s41562-021-01273-8 (supplementary material at https://osf.io/qsyvw/).

Jones, K. (1996) "Trust as an Affective Attitude," *Ethics*, 107(1), pp. 4–25. https://doi.org/10.1086/233694.

Keil, F. C. and Wilson, R. A. (2000) "The Shadows and Shallows of Explanation," in F. C. Keil and R. A. Wilson (eds.) *Minds and Machines*. MIT Press, pp. 137–159.

Keren, A. (2020) "Trust, Preemption, and Knowledge", in K. Dormandy, K. (ed.) *Trust in Epistemology*. Routledge, pp. 114–135.

Krishnamurthy, M., Liao, S-y, Deveaux, M., and Dalecki, M. (2017) "The Underrepresentation of Women in Prestigious Ethics Journals," *Hypatia*, 32 (4), pp. 928–939. https://doi.org/10.1111/hypa.12351.

Lagerspetz, M. (2021) "'The Grievance Studies Affair' Project: Reconstructing and Assessing the Experimental Design," *Science, Technology, & Human Values*, 46(2), pp. 402–424. https://doi.org/10.1177%2F0162243920923087.

Leiter, B. (2013) "Best Philosophy Publishers in English," *Leiter Reports: A Philosophy Blog*, February 5. https://leiterreports.typepad.com/blog/2013/02/best-philosophy-publishers-in-english.html (Accessed: December 31, 2021).

Levy, N. (2017) "Embodied Savoir-Faire: Knowledge-How Requires Motor Representations," *Synthese*, 194(2), pp. 511–530. https://doi.org/10.1007/s11229-015-0956-1.

Levy, N. (2021) *Bad Beliefs: Why They Happen to Good People*. Oxford University Press.

Levy, N. (2022) "In Trust We Trust: Epistemic Vigilance and Responsibility," *Social Epistemology*, 36(3), pp. 283–298. https://doi.org/10.1080/02691728.2022.2042420.

Lycan, W. (2009) "Giving Dualism Its Due," *Australasian Journal of Philosophy*, 87(4), pp. 551–563.

MacIntyre, A. (1990) *Three Rival Versions of Moral Enquiry*. University of Notre Dame Press. https://bit.ly/3OOmiEo (Accessed: August 8, 2023).

Mallapaty, S. (2018) "Paper Authorship Goes Hyper," *Nature Index*, January 30. www.natureindex.com/news-blog/paper-authorship-goes-hyper (Accessed: September 28, 2019).

Mascaro, O. and Sperber, D. (2009) "The Moral, Epistemic, and Mindreading Components of Children's Vigilance towards Deception," *Cognition*, 112(3), pp. 367–380. https://doi.org/10.1016/j.cognition.2009.05.012.

Melamed, Y. (2013) "Charitable Interpretations and the Political Domestication of Spinoza, or, Benedict in the Land of the Secular Imagination," in J. Smith, E. Schliesser, and M. Laerke (eds.) *Philosophy and Its History: Aims and Methods in the Study of Early Modern Philosophy*. Oxford University Press, pp. 258–277.

Nature (2021) "Editorial Criteria and Processes." www.nature.com/nature/for-authors/editorial-criteria-and-processes (Accessed: December 24, 2021).

O'Neill, O. (2020) "Questioning Trust," in J. Simon (ed.) *The Routledge Handbook of Trust and Philosophy*. Routledge.

Oxford University Press (2009) "FAQs" (Archive). https://global.oup.com/uk/archives/8.html# (Accessed: December 31, 2021).

Palus, S. (2015) "Is Double-Blind Review Better?," *APS News*, July. www.aps.org/publications/apsnews/201507/double-blind.cfm (Accessed: May 4, 2020).

Pennycook, G., Cheyne, J. A., Barr, N., Koehler, D. J., and Fugelsang, J. A. (2015) "On the Reception and Detection of Pseudo-Profound Bullshit," *Judgment and decision making*, 10, pp. 549–563 (supplementary material at https://sjdm.org/journal/15/15923a/supp.pdf).

Peters, D. P. and Ceci, S. J. (1982) "Peer-Review Practices of psychological Journals: The Fate of Published Articles, Submitted Again," *Behavioral and Brain Sciences*, 5(2), pp. 187–195. https://doi.org/10.1017/S0140525X000 11183.

Philosophical Review (2022) "Statistics – Last 12 Months." https://philosophi calreview.org/statistics (Accessed: June 4, 2022).

Plakias, A. (2019) "Publishing without Belief," *Analysis*, 79(4), pp. 638–646.

Plakias, A. (2023) "Publishing, Belief, and Self-Trust," *Episteme*, 20(3), pp. 632–646. https://doi.org/10.1017/epi.2022.41.

Pluckrose, H., Lindsay, J. A., and Boghossian, P. (2018) "Academic Grievance Studies and the Corruption of Scholarship,"*Areo*, October 2. https://areoma gazine.com/2018/10/02/academic-grievance-studies-and-the-corruption-of-scholarship/ (Accessed: August 8, 2023).

Pontille, D. and Torny, D. (2014) "The Blind Shall See! The Question of Anonymity in Journal Peer Review," *Ada: A Journal of Gender, New Media, and Technology*, 4. https://doi.org/10.7264/N3542KVW.

Price, P. C. and Stone, E. R. (2004) "Intuitive Evaluation of Likelihood Judgment Producers: Evidence for a Confidence Heuristic," *Journal of Behavioral Decision Making*, 17(1), pp. 39–57.

Pulford, B. D., Colman, A. M., Buabang, E. K., and Krockow, E. M. (2018) "The Persuasive Power of Knowledge: Testing the Confidence Heuristic," *Journal of Experimental Psychology: General*, 147(10), pp. 1431–1444. https://doi.org/10.1037/xge0000471.

Ritchie, S. (2020) *Science Fictions: Exposing Fraud, Bias, Negligence and Hype in Science*. Random House.

Rowbottom, D. P. (2022) "Peer Review May Not Be Such a Bad Idea: Response to Heesen and Bright," *British Journal for the Philosophy of Science* [pre-print]. https://doi.org/10.1086/714787.

Rozenblit, L. and Keil, F. (2002) "The Misunderstood Limits of Folk Science: An Illusion of Explanatory Depth," *Cognitive Science*, 26(5), pp. 521–562. https://doi.org/10.1207/s15516709cog2605_1.

Safi, M. (2014) "Journal Accepts Bogus Paper Requesting Removal from Mailing List," *The Guardian*, November 25. https://bit.ly/3QAW6yJ (Accessed: August 8, 2023).

Schliesser, E. (2013) "So, How Did Analysis Stack Up against Phil Review / JPhi / Mind (1995–8)?," *New APPS: Art, Politics, Philosophy, Science*, July 4. www.newappsblog.com/2013/07/so-how-did-analysis-stack-up-against-phil-reviewjphilmind-1995-8.html (Accessed: June 24, 2021).

Schwitzgebel, E. (2022) "Citation Rates by Academic Field: Philosophy Is Near the Bottom," *The Splintered Mind*, November 17. http://schwitzsplinters.blogspot .com/2022/11/citation-rates-by-academic-field.html (Accessed: December 9, 2022).

Science (2022) "Information for Authors." www.science.org/content/page/sci ence-information-authors#pct_faq (Accessed: December 24, 2021).

Shackel, N. (2005) "The Vacuity of Postmodernist Methodology," *Metaphilosophy*, 36(3), pp. 295–320. https://doi.org/10.1111/j.1467-9973.2005.00370.x.

Shema, H. (2014) "The Birth of Modern Peer Review," *Information Culture*, April 19. https://blogs.scientificamerican.com/information-culture/the-birth-of-modern-peer-review/.

Shieber, J. (2020) "Socially Distributed Cognition and the Epistemology of Testimony," in M. Fricker, P. J. Graham, D. Henderson, and N. J. L. L. Pedersen (eds.) *The Routledge Handbook of Social Epistemology*. Routledge, pp. 87–95. https://doi.org/10.4324/9781315717937-9.

Shtulman, A. (2006) "Qualitative Differences between Naïve and Scientific Theories of Evolution," *Cognitive Psychology*, 52(2), pp. 170–194. https:// doi.org/10.1016/j.cogpsych.2005.10.001.

Smith, B. (1992) "Derrida Degree: A Question of Honor," *The Times*, May 9.

Snodgrass, R. (2006) "Single- versus Double-Blind Reviewing: An Analysis of the Literature," ACM *SIGMOD Record*, 35(3), pp. 8–21. https://doi.org/ 10.1145/1168092.1168094.

Sokal, A. D. (1996a) "A Physicist Experiments with Cultural Studies," *Lingua Franca*, May/June. http://linguafranca.mirror.theinfo.org/9605/sokal.html (Accessed: January 28, 2022).

Sokal, A. D. (1996b) "Transgressing the Boundaries: Toward a Transformative Hermeneutics of Quantum Gravity," *Social Text*, 46(27), pp. 217–252.

Sperber, D. (2010) "The Guru Effect," *Review of Philosophy and Psychology*, 1 (4), pp. 583–592. https://doi.org/10.1007/s13164-010-0025-0.

Sperber, D., Clément, F., Heintz, C., *et al.* (2010) "Epistemic Vigilance," *Mind & Language*, 25(4), pp. 359–393. https://doi.org/10.1111/j.1468-0017.2010.01394.x.

Stanley, J. (2005) *Knowledge and Practical Interests*. Clarendon Press.

Stanley, J. (2015) *How Propaganda Works*. Princeton University Press. https://bit.ly/3ONBVfs (Accessed: August 8, 2023).

Stanley, J. (2018) *How Fascism Works: The Politics of Us and Them*. Random House.

Sterling, J., Jost, J., and Pennycook, G. (2016) "Are Neoliberals More Susceptible to Bullshit?," *Judgment and Decision Making*, 11, pp. 352–360.

Strawson, P. (1962) "Freedom and Resentment," *Proceedings of the British Academy*, 48, pp. 187–211. https://doi.org/10.1073/pnas.48.1.1.

Weinberg, J. (2018) "The 'Insanely Low Acceptance Rates' of Philosophy Journals," *Daily Nous*, May 24. https://dailynous.com/2018/05/24/insanely-low-acceptance-rates-philosophy-journals/ (Accessed: December 24, 2021).

Weisberg, D. S., Keil, F. C., Goodstein, J., Rawson, E., and Gray, J. R. (2008) "The Seductive Allure of Neuroscience Explanations," *Journal of Cognitive Neuroscience*, 20(3), pp. 470–477. https://doi.org/10.1162/jocn.2008.20040.

Wilhelm, I., Conklin, S. L., and Hassoun, N. (2018) "New Data on the Representation of Women in Philosophy Journals: 2004–2015," *Philosophical Studies*, 175(6), pp. 1441–1464. https://doi.org/10.1007/s11098-017-0919-0.

Wittgenstein (1965) "A Lecture on Ethics," *Philosophical Review*, 74, pp. 3–12.

Acknowledgments

I am grateful to two anonymous reviewers for very helpful, and complementary, guidance on improving this Element. Helen De Cruz, Alex Plakias, Rob Ross, and Eric Schliesser pointed me to literature I should be aware of and gaps in my thinking. I also owe Stephen Hetherington thanks for encouragement. Section 3 contains material originally published in Levy (2022). I gratefully acknowledge the support of the John Templeton Foundation (grant 62631) and of the Wellcome Trust (grant WT104848).

Epistemology

Stephen Hetherington

University of New South Wales, Sydney

Stephen Hetherington is Professor Emeritus of Philosophy at the University of New South Wales, Sydney. He is the author of numerous books including *Knowledge and the Gettier Problem* (Cambridge University Press, 2016), and *What Is Epistemology?* (Polity, 2019), and is the editor of, most recently, *Knowledge in Contemporary Epistemology* (with Markos Valaris: Bloomsbury, 2019), and *What the Ancients Offer to Contemporary Epistemology* (with Nicholas D. Smith: Routledge, 2020). He was the Editor-in-Chief of the *Australasian Journal of Philosophy* from 2013 until 2022.

About the Series

This Elements series seeks to cover all aspects of a rapidly evolving field, including emerging and evolving topics such as: fallibilism; knowinghow; self-knowledge; knowledge of morality; knowledge and injustice; formal epistemology; knowledge and religion; scientific knowledge; collective epistemology; applied epistemology; virtue epistemology; wisdom. The series demonstrates the liveliness and diversity of the field, while also pointing to new areas of investigation.

Cambridge Elements ☰

Epistemology

Elements in the Series

Printed in the United States
by Baker & Taylor Publisher Services